The
Unwanted
Son

by
Benuel M. Fisher

The Unwanted Son
by Benuel M. Fisher

Artwork on front and back covers
suggested by the author
Paintings by Emma Stoltzfus

Published by:
Benuel M. Fisher
722A Peters Road
New Holland, PA 17557

First printing October 2003
Second printing December 2003
Third printing February 2004
Fourth printing March 2011
Fifth printing April 2017

Printed in the United States of America

The Unwanted Son

Stories About Lester Getz

	Page
Preface	v

*

The Getz Family	1
A New Baby	2
Living in Christ Lapp's Tenant House	3
Smallpox Vaccination and Diphtheria	6

*

Samuel's Death	8
No Good-byes	9

*

A Long, Lonely Ride	11
Hard Work on the Farm	12
"Run, Run, Run!"	15
Raw Potatoes	18
Thunderstorms	21
Alone in the Woods	24
Thanksgiving Morning	27

*

God said, "Run!"	29
Back to School	30
Threshing Wheat	32

*

Locating Mother	35
Moving Home	37
Planting a Garden	40
The Boys Need a Whipping	42

*

Learning to Sew	47
Working at the Sewing Factory	48
Working at the Cigar Factory	50
Butchering the Turkey	52

❊❂❊

Lester Trips on a Stumbling Block 55

❊❂❊

Life Goes On..58
A New Car 60
Drafted for War 61
Sunday School 62
A New Trade 63
Bartending 64

❊❂❊

Mother's Death 67

❊❂❊

A Homeless Family...68
Remodeling House 68
Selling Beauty-Rest® Mattresses 71

❊❂❊

Losing His Home 73
Working with Alcoholics 75
Rutt's Furniture 77
Recognizing Another Stumbling Block 78
Saving a Business 79

❊❂❊

Facing a Man with a Gun 82
Never Refuse the Work of the Lord............84

❊❂❊

Marriage 90
End of a Job 92
Working at Gimbels 92
Another Job 94
Working at Gimbels Again 97
Another Phase of Life 98
Retirement? 100

❊❂❊

Stories About Hobos
Scared by a Hobo (Tramp) 105
When Hobos Walked the Roads 108

Preface

I became acquainted with the story of the unwanted boy in March 2001, when my 87-year-old father, Amos C. Fisher, was in a hospital in Lancaster, Pennsylvania, as a colectomy patient. One evening while my two sisters visited him, they sang some beautiful old German hymns.

Betty Getz was walking by Dad's room but stopped in amazement to listen to singing such as she had never heard before. Curious to know more, she entered the room and visited with my dad and sisters. She told them her husband, Lester, was a patient only a few rooms down the hall. Later that evening my sisters stopped in to meet Lester, who was 88 years old.

Lester soon began telling them about how he had had such a hard life as a little boy. After his father died, his mother gave him away to a harsh, rough farmer who verbally and physically abused him. Lester was often whipped for not getting enough work done or for not doing it right. At the age of nine, he ran away and lived alone in the woods for several months. Lester talked and talked of his sad life and how, through earnest prayer, God had helped him all his life.

The life of this old Christian man touched my sisters' hearts quite deeply. Later, they related this story to me, and something inside told me I must meet this man and hear his life story. I thought if all his sorrows were healed through prayer and faith, it would be worthwhile writing a book. People could use Lester's life story as a lesson and realize that God hears prayers, even the prayers of the forsaken.

After my father passed away in June of 2002, I visited Lester and his wife. Soon he began talking of his life. I wrote short notes as fast as my fingers could write. Within an hour, Lester was nearly too tired to say anymore. He was on oxygen 24-hours a day to support his breathing.

When he mentioned Rachel Miller and Christ Lapp, my interest was sparked. Rachel was my mother! Now, for sure, I needed to know more and made plans to visit Lester again.

One night soon after that first visit, Lester had a dream. In his dream God revealed to him that someone should publish his life in a book. The next day he told Betty of his dream.

She said, "It will make me too tired to write all that."

Lester said, "God will help us."

So for the next three weeks Lester repeated the story of his life, and Betty wrote it, in short form, a few pages every day.

Meanwhile, one night I lay awake for a long time. Sleep wouldn't come and I got to thinking of Lester Getz's hard life. Since I had published one book, I had a small desire to write another book, but I thought, "This is too complicated for me unless I have a lot more information, and Lester gets too tired from talking."

Suddenly, my mind went blank—not as in a dream or a vision—and then a few moments later I came to my senses and somehow I knew I should write a book for those old folks.

Some weeks later, my wife, Mary, and I visited Lester and Betty at their home in Lititz, Pennsylvania. Once again Lester started relating his life, and then Betty handed me 72 pages of notes she had written over the past few weeks.

Those notes were a big help to me, but her handwriting sometimes kept me guessing. After three or four readings, however, I managed to determine quite well what it all represented. So although the things included in this book did happen to Lester, I added background details and the wording of conversations between people to make this a story rather than just a collection of facts.

Lester and I felt our getting together was more than a coincidence, and when we compared notes we felt our command and desire to put this story in a book came in the same week or maybe the same day and night. Did God really plan it this way?

So I fully decided to try my hand at writing with help from above. I wanted it to be a book of good moral reading.

Lester's life was hard. He made the best of every circumstance and in this way, I feel, he was God's servant. Many times he could have complained, but he didn't.

My desire is that this book will be a great help to the reader who has to deal with problems such as Lester had. Hopefully, you will not have all of them. If you do, take the same route as he did, have faith in prayer, and God will help you too.

I give all honor to God for helping me write these stories based on true facts.

Please note that Lester was almost 90 years old when he told me the story of his life. At times I was not sure I fully understood some of the situations he was describing. Also, sometimes memories differ slightly from the actual facts that happened many years earlier. For this reason I ask your forgiveness if some of the names, facts, and details in this story are inaccurate.

Benuel M. Fisher

Books by Benual M. Fisher

The Unwanted Son (2003)

The Forsaken Child (2005)

Everlasting Strength (2007)

Uncle Benny and His Brother (2008)

Just a Hired Boy (Knecht) (2009)

Coming Home Again (2010)

The Shepherd Survives (2011)

God's Special Children (2012)

Welsh Mountain Survivors (2013)

Kansas Prairie Doctor (2014)

Slave Girls Escaping (2016)

Available from the Author

Benuel M. Fisher
722 A Peters Road
New Holland, PA 17557
717-354-4084

The Getz Family

The sun shone brightly in the eastern sky that late May morning. Strawberries, potatoes, peas, carrots, and red beets were growing abundantly in a half-acre vegetable garden. Flowers bloomed and sparkled in the morning dew, and soft breezes wafted their fragrance through the open windows of an old gray house along Rettew Mill Road near Meadow Valley Church in Ephrata Township, Lancaster County, Pennsylvania.

The folks who rented the gray house for $5 a month, Samuel and Susanna Getz, were poor. Clothes were handed down from child to child until they were worn to rags. Shoes were not worn by family members if the weather was fit to go barefoot.

The garden created plenty of work. Five days a week Samuel and at least some of his 12 children planted all kinds of vegetables, hoed and pulled weeds, and throughout the summer and fall months harvested the mature and ripened produce to feed the family and to sell at market.

Susanna canned and stored away a good supply of the fruits and vegetables for winter use. Even so, it took nearly everything they could save to pay their rent and feed and clothe the big family.

Every Friday Susanna baked 40 pies to be sold at the market on Saturday. Many of the windows in the Getz home did not have screens. In summer months when the wood- and coal-fired kitchen-range heated up the house, there was a choice—keep the flies out or open the windows and let the heat out. As pie dough was rolled out on the kitchen table with a wobbly old rolling pin, who knew if flies plunged into the pie filling. If they did, they were soon well baked in the hot oven of the kitchen range.

Saturday was market day. Early in the morning, Samuel hitched "Prince," the horse, to the spring wagon and headed to Ephrata. There along Main Street he tied Prince to a post and displayed his produce—vegetables, pies, butter, cheese, and eggs. Sometimes Susanna dressed a few chickens to send along. Quite often a few of the children went along with Samuel, thereby freeing Susanna from the need to keep an eye on all the youngsters.

A New Baby

The Getz kitchen was already getting hot when the sun beamed its first bright rays into the windows on Friday, May 23, 1913. Susanna had started her pies before daylight and wanted to get them baked before noon. As the kitchen grew warmer she, with good reason, became tired and irritable and started snapping at the children.

Lester Grant Getz, Susanna's eight-pound baby, took his first breath at 3:00 p.m. in the family bedroom. The aroma of 40 freshly-baked pies filled his nostrils immediately.

Lester was the thirteenth child of Samuel Feather Getz— the third child of his union with Susanna. Samuel's first wife had died during the birth of their tenth child, daughter Ella. That was quite a hard blow, and with ten children to raise, he knew he needed help. Hiring Susanna as a housekeeper and later marrying her relieved him of the burden of raising his children alone, but life was still hard for a man in the early 1900's when money was scarce.

Susanna had a two-month-old child when Samuel hired her as a housekeeper. The man who had fathered her child had been put in jail and her marriage to him had been cancelled.

Susanna proved to be a good mother to Samuel's ten children, so after two years as his housekeeper, they were married. Two years later Florence was born. This was a joy to have a daughter together. Two years later Nathan, Samuel's twelfth child, arrived and he was the baby of the family for seven years.

Susanna was quite happy to have children of her own.

2

The others were her stepchildren and although some were already married and away from home, she had plenty of work—getting ready for market plus keeping house and cooking, and sewing for the large family.

Lester was born seven years after Nathan. Susanna had not wanted another child and from the beginning, she neglected him and never fully accepted him. She continued to treat Nathan as her baby and never treated Lester fairly even as a small child. His father, however, dearly loved him and was happy with him.

Many times God has a way planned where one person's life, through trials and suffering, can benefit other people and help them become Christians. The life of Lester Getz reveals the great love of God for a small, unwanted boy and how Lester returned that love to God and to others throughout the years of his life.

The lives of Adam and Eve are history but can be of benefit to all Christians. The life story of Joseph, a young boy sold as a slave, is also history. The love and teachings of Jesus are history. What valuable history occurs today? Is it still necessary to write history at this time when we think Jesus is coming any day and will put an end to time?

Living in Christ Lapp's Tenant House

Before Lester was a year old, his parents moved into Christ Lapp's tenant house along Horseshoe Road near Heller's Church in Upper Leacock Township, Lancaster County.

Samuel and Susanna attended different churches before their marriage, and while Samuel preferred to continue with the Brethren church, Susanna wanted to stay with the Reformed denomination and dress in accord with their practices. She never yielded to Samuel's wishes that she join his church, but with their children they attended church every Sunday—one Sunday at Heller's Church and the next Sunday at Monterey. They could walk to Heller's, but they drove the horse and carriage to Monterey.

Every Saturday evening the Getz children took a bath— one at a time. During the summer and fall months, the baths

3

were taken on the back porch in the pump trough. In wintertime the children bathed in a bucket of warm water behind the wood stove in the kitchen.

The Getz family was a Christian family where the children were taught, during their young years, to believe in God and in prayer. Susanna faithfully went along upstairs with the children at bedtime and taught them to kneel to pray, the same as Samuel's first wife had done. Samuel always prayed at breakfast, Susanna prayed at the noon meal, and Samuel prayed again at supper. Although Lester's mother was not always kind to him, he remembers praying that she might accept him better.

Samuel had convictions about not working on Sunday and did not allow his wife to cook a meal that day. She had to prepare it on Saturday.

Sunday afternoons were filled with neighborhood fun—Amish and English neighbors together. The men and boys occasionally played corner ball out in a straw-covered barnyard while the women visited together, sharing their joys and sorrows. Although of different faiths, there was little difference in their ways of living. Lester especially enjoyed accompanying his dad on Sunday afternoon visits to Christ Lapp's house. He admired that Amish man a lot.

While Samuel's family lived in the Lapp tenant house, Samuel worked for Christ for a dollar a day. Lester often went along to help do whatever he could. He was a respectful lad, full of energy, and took a great interest in farming. Often Christ would give him a piece of candy or a pretzel. Lester also enjoyed working for Lavina, Christ's wife, in the vegetable garden and flower beds. He knew she loved him better than his own mother did.

At age six Lester learned how to harness a horse and sometimes drove a team of two horses hitched to the tobacco wagon while Christ stood on the wagon tongue. After a few days of practice, he was able to drive the team alone and occasionally stayed home from school to do farm work—which he liked better than school work.

Christ Lapp was a good manager and had a well-kept

farm. Everything was neat and in order. He farmed four acres of tobacco plus lots of vegetables, and had two pens of Rhode Island Red chickens, two Guernsey cows, and six hogs. The Lapps butchered hogs, put the meat in crocks, and poured hot lard over the top to seal it. This way the meat would not spoil. Every Saturday morning Christ loaded the market wagon with homemade butter, milk, eggs, vegetables, baked goods, and meat and drove to Lancaster Market where he found eager buyers for his farm-fresh food.

Lester remembers hearing Christ say he had wished for three sons and had dreams of buying three farms and seeing his sons as successful farmers someday. Five of the Lapps' eight children died young and only two sons, Christ and John, and one daughter grew to adulthood. The parents wished to see their children continue in the same lifestyle as themselves, but as often happens, this did not prove to be the way.

Christ's son, Christ, Jr., farmed for some years but did not appear to be successful. One incident my mother recalled was that at one time he had only two cows to milk and bought two automatic milkers so he didn't need to milk by hand. Years later he and his family left the Amish Church. His sons proved to be quite successful in a restaurant business.

Son John later farmed the home farm but became afflicted with a mental illness. He was a patient at Harrisburg State Hospital for many years until his death in 1970. His wife, Susie, visited him every week and took his clothing home to wash. Meanwhile, Susie, with a hired man to help, kept the farm going. She had two little girls to care for in addition to the farm work.

The Lapps' one daughter, Mary, stayed single until late in life when she married a widower, Christ E. Stoltzfus.

Quite often God has plans for a family different than what the parents have. So it was with this family who, after laying some of their little children in their graves, shared their love with Lester, who, with no brothers or sisters near his age, enjoyed playing with the Lapp children.

One November Christ and Lavina Lapp invited their neighbors, the Samuel Getz family, over to share their

Thanksgiving meal with them. Lavina roasted a big rooster and left the legs on, toes and all. When the roast was put on the table, the legs of the rooster were straight up.

Three-year-old Lester laughed and yelled, "Look at the legs! Even the toenails are still on!"

His older brothers mocked him a bit for raising such a fuss, but Christ Lapp defended him saying, "That's all right; he is only a little boy yet."

❦

Smallpox Vaccination and Diphtheria

All children needed to be vaccinated for smallpox before starting school, so Lester was vaccinated sometime during the summer before he was to start his first term. Somehow his arm became quite infected, and because his parents were poor, they did not take him back to the doctor right away. When Samuel finally took Lester to the doctor, the doctor said, "I will treat it, but I might have to take the arm off if it does not heal."

"No, you will not take off my son's arm," Samuel said. "I never raised a crippled child and I will not now either. I will take him home and take care of it myself."

Samuel remembered a home remedy and when they got home he said, "Susanna, go up to the attic and bring down a big piece of *speck* (fat)."

Susanna brought down one of the home-cured pieces of meat and Samuel cut off a few slices of *speck* and wrapped them around Lester's arm. Within a week the infection was nearly gone, so because of a home remedy, Lester's arm was saved and Samuel was saved from a costly doctor bill.

God had a reason for healing that arm. Lester used it for many good deeds throughout his life.

Home remedies were used for many different illnesses, but some illnesses could not be conquered. Diphtheria was one that often, within a short period of time, took the life of one or more members of the same family, leaving sad, aching hearts. The disease was very contagious, often occurring in winter when houses were closed up and people spent more time shut in together.

6

Neighbors to the Samuel Getz family got diphtheria. The Getz family did not have this illness and stayed away from the stricken family. Other neighbors did the same. When Samuel learned that two of the children had died within a few days of each other, he said, "We must bury them."

Susanna said, "You can't! Think of your own children. In a few days our family will come down with the same thing. Stay away."

"We will pray about it and see what God says," Samuel said.

That night, six-year-old Lester, who shared a bedroom in the small house with some of his older sisters, sneaked out of the room and listened while his parents prayed about the situation. For once, his older sisters didn't catch him sneaking out. He heard his parents agree that God wanted his father to bury the two dead neighbor children.

The next morning Samuel dressed in old clothes taken from the rag box. He hitched his horse to Christ Lapp's spring wagon, drove to the neighbor's home, and loaded the two small corpses from their porch. He then drove away. Digging the grave in the frozen ground must have been quite a chore. Lester never learned where the bodies were buried.

Susanna watched for Samuel's return, and before dark she saw him coming at a distance. She took all the children into another room to keep them from watching him as he parked the wagon along side of the barn and then took off his clothes and burned them. To keep any germs from spreading from him to any of the buildings, he next took a bath outside in the cold. The wagon was left outside for three weeks until the rains washed it off a few times. He took every precaution possible to protect his family from this sickness.

Lester, who had heard his parents pray about the situation, later questioned his dad about why he had buried the children.

Samuel told him the above details and said, "What God tells you to do, you must do."

Samuel's Death

On Samuel's sixty-ninth birthday, Susanna and her daughter Minnie Ellen prepared dinner for 104 guests. She always enjoyed celebrating her husband's birthday on July 4 and invited many friends. Lester was aware that she always had lots of ambition to do things that interested her, but she still had no interest in caring for and treating him, her youngest son, as a mother normally would.

The neighbor children all looked forward to a visit from Pappy Getz at Christmas, because each year Samuel filled bags for them with the same items the Getz children all received—an orange, a hard-boiled egg stained with onion shells, and two pieces of candy. The Getz children received their gifts on their breakfast plate.

At age 69 Samuel filled 20 bags and set out on Christmas morning to share his love with the neighbor children. His daughter Carrie was preparing the noontime Christmas dinner at her home. When Samuel didn't arrive, Nathan went to look for him. He soon came back saying, "Dad is at home on the floor rolling around in great pain."

Carrie's husband, Roy, went to get a doctor, who left his Christmas dinner and took Samuel to the hospital. He had a rupture which had burst and knotted his bowels. Gangrene soon set in and he died on New Year's Day.

It snowed most of the day of the funeral and at places it was hard to find the road as Christ Lapp took some of the Getz family from Heller's Church to Voganville in a two-horse sled. During the approximately nine-mile trip, he had to go through the fields occasionally. Many folks arrived in sleighs and the church house was so full that people had to stand outside in the snow.

Although young, Lester had already learned that God

doesn't always answer prayers the way we want Him to, and he grieved deeply at the death of his loving father. He was quite aware of how harshly his mother treated him and feared his life might change drastically. His hope was that he could rely on Christ Lapp as a replacement for his father. Christ would have adopted him, but Susanna would not allow it. She apparently did not care to have her unwanted son live nearby or see him as a happy boy.

No Good-byes

The sale of Samuel Getz's personal property, which consisted of shop tools and farm-related items, was held in March. Lester had a feeling something unusual would happen and kept hold of his beloved, faithful dog, "Shep." Finally, the dog he loved and even the chain were sold. Lester cried to no avail.

When the sale was over, Lester saw his mother and a man walking from the house toward him. She had a box in her hand and said, "Lester, you are going with this man."

The man took the box and Lester's mother turned around and walked toward the house without another word or a backward look.

Lester watched her for a moment then turned and walked away with the complete stranger. He longed for Shep, his beloved dog, but Shep had been sold and was gone. None of his brothers or sisters were in sight as he got into the stranger's vehicle, so there were no good-byes. He had no idea where he was going, and tears ran down his cheeks. He wished he had known what was going to happen, because he would have gone to Christ Lapp and kept out of sight of his mother. He was homesick for his dad. He hoped he would have a good home with this man, but it turned out to be quite the opposite.

Lester had no idea how long he would have to stay at the stranger's house, and he had no idea if he would ever come home or see his brothers and sisters again. No explanation was given about the move and he discovered the box contained only one set of clothes. All his toys, the things he had received as gifts, and all his other personal belongings were left behind.

All his life, Lester wondered why his mother did not love him. Even though she had not wanted another baby, why had she never learned to love and admire him? He was respectful and had worked hard at whatever she asked him to do.

Often the youngest in a family is spoiled and pampered, but apparently Susanna was tired of caring for her unwanted little boy. Perhaps she hoped to remarry and enjoy life without the burden of this young boy.

Although she had dishonored her husband by being unwilling to give up her church after their marriage, she had taught the children to pray at bedtime.

God seemed to be the only One who needed Lester, and throughout his life he tried to be His honorable servant. He later remembered his father telling the Old Testament story of Joseph who had been sold by his brothers as a slave to the Ishmaelites. Joseph was 17 years old when that happened — Lester Getz was only eight.

A Long, Lonely Ride

The late afternoon sun was lost in clouds, and the air grew quite cold as Lester and the strange man, Frank, drove through territory unfamiliar to Lester. They drove and drove and Lester lost all sense of direction—he only knew he was far from home.

Glances at Frank's stern face quelled any questions Lester wanted to ask. He wanted to cry, but instead he prayed silently while Frank chewed on a big wad of tobacco and mumbled to himself.

Finally, they drove in a long, bumpy lane which Lester later learned was in the West Willow area. Frank carried the box of Lester's clothes to the house, ordering him to follow. Frank's wife greeted him with a hello, but made no extra comments. Lester was not included in the conversation during supper and he heard no mention of the sale or questions about why Frank had brought him along home. He sensed his move had been planned in advance. He felt sick. He wasn't hungry and the food had no taste.

After supper he was shown a room upstairs where he was to sleep, and without as much as a "good night," he was left alone. The hardest day of his young life ended with thoughts about how he could ever accept this hardship.

The next morning Lester was aroused before dawn. His days of hard work from sunrise until sunset had begun. Although by Pennsylvania law a boy his age should be in school, there was no more school for eight-year-old Lester— the subject was not even mentioned. There were no children to talk to, and he soon learned not to ask questions. Frank and his wife had no time for anything except work on the farm in the busy spring season.

Without a mother's love, Lester's life had been rather

unpleasant and empty after his dad's death on New Year's Day. Frank's place, however, was many, many times worse. He lived practically in solitude with no friendly words or praise to encourage him. If his work was not done as Frank expected, he was sent to bed without supper. Often he got a licken instead of supper.

Since he had to work every day including Sunday, it wasn't long before he lost track of the days. By not going to school or church, every day seemed the same. He missed going to church. Although his mother had quit going to church after his dad died, Lester's brothers and sisters had quite often taken him along with them. He often thought of Christ Lapp and how he had loved to work for him. He thought of running away and going to live with Christ, but he had no idea which way to go or where he might find the Lapp home.

Lester talked to the only One he knew could hear him. He prayed and prayed to God, asking that Frank would be kinder and more patient. Many nights he cried himself to sleep.

Hard Work on the Farm

Day after day Lester was ordered to plow with three horses hitched to a walking plow. If the plow hit a rock, it was pushed out of the furrow and Lester's 50-pound body could not drag the plow back into the furrow again. His 180-pound boss could easily handle the plow and horses and he harshly demanded Lester do his work right.

The plow most used on farms in the early 1900's weighed a possible 125 pounds and had two wooden handles to guide it. Whenever the plow hit a big rock, the handles were yanked out of Lester's hands. The rocks plowed out were to be carried to the end of the field and laid along the fence row. Lester did not have the strength to carry the heaviest rocks and learned to dread Frank's reaction.

"I told you to carry the rocks along the fence and you disobeyed me again. You will get a whipping again tonight," were the harsh words he heard and that is what happened—a whipping plus going to bed without supper.

Lester had no choice but to try to obey whatever his boss

asked, but many nights he crept to his room weary and hungry. There he fell on his knees beside his bed and tried to pray as his mother had taught him. Night after night he asked God to deliver him out of his misery, then trusting that God had heard him, he crawled into bed and soon fell asleep. Each morning God gave him strength to go on again, but no matter how hard he tried to please Frank, he never received any praise. Frank only treated him with rudeness and cruelty.

One day Lester noticed the April page was torn off the calendar, so he figured it might be the first day of May. The sunny, warmer days seemed to affirm his idea. He kept track of each new day and hoped his sister Florence might send him a birthday card on May 23. Even while hoping she would send him a card, he doubted that Frank would give it to him if it came. He also wondered if his mother had even told his brothers and sisters where he was. When the day he figured was his birthday came and went without a word from anyone, he decided he was now nine years old and that his days of play and childhood were over. It looked, to him, as though every day from then on would only mean more work.

His workday started at 4:00 a.m. during the wheat harvest in July and he was expected to do the same hard work as Frank. The work was strenuous and the hours seemed endless. The hot sun beat mercilessly as he laid sheaves, layer-upon-layer on the wagon while his energetic boss rapidly pitched them up to him with a two-prong fork. Harsh words frequently cut through the hot, dusty air, "Lay them sheaves down properly so they won't slide off. You know what will happen tonight if . . ."

Lester had an awful fear of that whip being slapped across his back. He had never done this job on Christ Lapp's farm, but suddenly, without being taught, he was supposed to know all about it.

He often thought of the words his father had said about burying the two children who died of diphtheria. "What God tells you to do, you must do." Frank was no God, but Lester still thought he should obey him. If his mother was being paid for his work, he felt he must do whatever was asked of him, and he didn't dare ask any questions.

Later when Frank unloaded the wagon in the barn, he forked the sheaves up into the mow where, in the 90° or more heat, Lester worked as fast as he could, spreading them in layers. He knew he soon better get the knack of doing the job.

He wore the same sweaty clothes every day; the wheat dust stuck to his unwashed body, making him itchy and irritable. After three days of this hard work, his strength was nearly drained. It was nearly dark the evening of that third day when, as they drove a big wagon load of sheaves toward the barn, Frank said, "We will wait 'til tomorrow morning to unload."

Just as the horses pulled the wagon onto the barn bank, half of the load started sliding off. Frank yelled at the horses and kept going until the wagon was inside the barn. He was terribly angry at Lester for not having done a better job of loading the wheat sheaves.

The horses were unhitched and fed, and the two tired workers did the other barn chores.

Then as Frank's fury grew, he forked the sheaves, two at a time, into the barn and then up into the mow. "Come on, buddy, get them layered. It's getting dark," he yelled.

Hungry and near exhaustion, Lester continued working. As quickly as he could, he laid the sheaves side-by-side in layers. In the hot strawmow the sweat dripped off the innocent castaway child.

When the job was done, the barn doors were closed. Lester dreaded what might take place next and he was right. He groaned in agony and tears sprang from his blue eyes as hard blows, from a powerful hand, hit his weary back. The noon meal was a long-forgotten memory to his empty stomach and although he saw the table prepared for the evening meal, he was ordered to bed without supper.

Weak and miserable Lester wished for the comfort of a good bath, a good supper for his hungry stomach, and true love from just anybody. He got none of these. After his lonely prayers, he lay down to sleep.

Too tired and hungry to sleep, he got up and went on his knees again. He prayed and prayed, for a long time, asking

God why he needed to stay at this place with unfriendly, harsh folks. He wondered if he could go back to his mother. Surely that would be better than this lonely misery. He could not control his tears as he thought of his dear father up in heaven, and cried, "Please, Jesus, may I go to be with my dad this very night?"

"Run, Run, Run!"

Everything was quiet downstairs. Frank was sound asleep, and Lester wondered if he could possibly sneak down to find something to satisfy his hunger. That would be an act of open disobedience, however, and Lester knew what would happen if Frank caught him. So he decided against that plan.

The bedroom windows were open that humid, warm, July night. Lester had no idea what time of the night it might be as he again knelt and prayed earnestly for God to deliver him from this place where he had spent nearly four months. It seemed as though he heard the words, "Run, run, run," inside his head.

"Yes, I'm going to go," he decided and quietly got into his sweaty, dirty bib-overalls.

The decision was made as he stepped out the window onto the porch roof, hoping he wouldn't fall. Carefully he twisted his tired body forward over the edge of the roof and, with both hands, grabbed a porch post.

Often he had wished there was a dog on the farm that he could have for a friend. Now as he quietly slid to the ground, he was glad there was no dog around to arouse Frank.

He had asked God to lead him in the right direction, and he set off running, empty handed, out through the fields in the quiet moonlight night. As he passed a few wild apple trees, he filled his bib-overalls with whatever apples came into his hands and then ran on. Soon he came to a woods and somehow felt this is where God wanted him to stay.

Under the trees the leaves shaded the light of the moon, making it quite dark. At last he decided he was far enough into the woods for it to be safe to lie down. He rested his weary body against a big tree and munched down a few apples to satisfy his awful hunger.

The crickets were ending their night humming when Lester relaxed and stretched his weary body on the bare, cool earth. "Dare I go to sleep?" he wondered.

As he drifted off to sleep, his thoughts wandered to a minister's sermon about someone named John who lived alone in a desert. John's only source of food had been locusts and wild honey.

Long after daybreak the sound of a mocking bird, calling in a high tone, awoke the still drowsy little boy. Lester leaped to his feet as fear gripped him. "Where am I?"

His first thought was of Frank, but after a careful search of each direction, he calmed enough to remember his nighttime flight into the woods. Next he felt the familiar pangs of thirst and hunger and searched his pockets for another apple. By the light of day he saw it was wormy, but he figured that if the four he had eaten the night before hadn't made him sick, these probably wouldn't either.

Being careful to make no noise, Lester crept deeper into the woods. His spirits rose when he spied a small brook, its bright clear water meandering under leafy bushes. "Well, I have no cup to drink out of," he whispered to himself and stretched out on his belly to drink from the refreshing cool stream.

Wormy apples and water from the stream relieved his physical agony for the moment, but fear of Frank haunted him. "What if someone sees me and makes me go back?" he agonized. "I must hide somewhere."

His eyes searched his surroundings and saw, a few yards from the stream, quite a few bushes had branches that hung close to the ground. He pulled off more stout branches and made a little hideout. Surveying his handiwork, he thought, "Surely no one will find me here in this hideout."

Throughout the day Lester sat alone in his leafy hideout. He thought with fear and dread about Frank and his cruelty. Then he thought about God and things he had heard in church over the years. "Is this where God led me—beside the still waters? I never was in such a peaceful place before."

Suddenly, he remembered that he had forgotten to say his morning prayers. "What shall I pray?" He asked himself.

"I know, I will ask God to take care of me the way He did when He sent ravens to Elijah the prophet with food every day while he sat beside a small brook."

The peace of God descended upon Lester as it had never done before. Weary and tired from the strenuous days of hard work he had endured, he soon lay down in his shelter and went to sleep. No one but God knew where Lester was.

Late in the afternoon he woke up feeling well rested but hungry. Cautiously, watching every step to avoid crunching twigs, he searched around. He was afraid to go more than a few yards beyond his leafy abode, but hoped he could find something to eat while it was still daylight—wild apples or berries. He was sure he could find nothing in the dark at night. "Surely if God led me here, He will not let me starve," he thought. "Will He show me some wild honey or locusts as He did for John the Baptist?"

Fear of being seen drove Lester back into his little shelter to wait for darkness to hide and protect him. His thoughts wandered here and there as he listened to the sweet music of insects echoing through the woods. Their cheery sounds drove away some of his loneliness. But he worried about what and where he might find something to eat. His stomach told him he needed to eat soon.

At dusk Lester felt a strong urge to be clean, and he decided to take a bath in the little, five-inches-deep stream of water. He first tried to eliminate his hunger with long drinks of the cool water, and then, without soap, washcloth, or towel, he took a bath. "This is how the Indians did," he thought. With his body washed clean of the sweat and dust of many days of work in the fields, he longed for clean clothes. There was only one thing to do—wash his bib-overalls, shirt, and underpants in the stream. Naked and alone, with his clothing drying on nearby bushes, Lester felt forlorn, forsaken, and rejected by everyone. He had no home, no friends, no food, not even shoes—only a little hideout in a forest.

He did not know what day it was, but he clung to the peace of God and the assurance that God would not let him starve. He depended on that.

Raw Potatoes

The fear of being caught was tremendous. Lester could well imagine Frank's wrath and angry words when he discovered his hired help wasn't around to load wheat that morning. He figured Frank knew quite well why he had run off, and he wondered if Frank had notified his mother that her little, nine-year-old son was missing. Maybe even the police and neighbors were looking for him!

Little time is wasted if a child is lost or missing now. A report goes out quickly, and immediately many volunteers leave their jobs to help search for the lost one. In 1943 a little four-year-old girl was lost in the woods of the Blue Ridge Mountains. Hundreds of people searched five days, through all kinds of underbrush, until finally she was found alive high up in the mountains.

No one at the Getz home along Heller's Church Road knew what had happened to the little cast-out son. His mother never went to check on him at Frank's place, but, oh how Lester wished his brothers would come searching for him. He learned later that if anyone inquired about his absence from home, they were told, by his mother, that he was away working for a farmer.

Being alone in the woods with only God to talk to, Lester felt close to Him. Listening to the singing of all kinds of birds, smelling the sweet fragrance of honeysuckle, watching the colorful butterflies, and hearing the unending rasping chorus of the locusts became almost like a church service to Lester. One of the few joys of his long, four months at Frank's home had been attending church once—the only time Frank and his wife had gone while he was there. How Lester had enjoyed that sermon—it was the one pleasure he had to think about as he sat hidden in his leafy abode under the trees that day.

Judging from the slant of the hazy setting sun, Lester figured the direction his shelter faced. He had no remembrance, however, of which direction he had run after climbing out of his bedroom window or how far he might be from Frank's farm. Nothing looked familiar—everything was new and strange.

All day as Lester rested, one thought bothered him. The birds and wild creatures knew where to look for their own food — they survive summer and winter. "God supplies food for them," he thought. "Will He also care for me? What can I find to eat?"

As daylight faded he again considered his problem. He saw no fruit trees in his little area of the woods. Although a few rabbits hopped about, Lester had no way to catch any, and no knife to skin one if he caught one.

"Must I die here in the woods? Is this my punishment for running away from Frank?" A confused assortment of thoughts ran through his young brain.

Many times that day he crept to the stream and, down on his belly tried to quench his hunger by drinking water.

Twilight turned the woods into shadows. He felt lonely and once again knelt to recite his evening prayers. "God, I'm hungry," he prayed to the God he had been taught was like a merciful father. "Lead me to a place where I may find something to eat."

He felt that God had heard his earnest plea and sensed a serene quietness all around him. He became calm. Again his thoughts flowed high above the treetops, on up to heaven where his dad was.

Assured that God was with him, he got out of his hut and quietly began walking northward. As he approached a clearing, the bright moon was ascending over the horizon. How beautiful this looked. Never before in all his days had he noticed this wonderful light at night as he did now, but it cast fear into his heart. "This is too much light. If Frank is looking for me, he could easily see me — maybe before I see him," he thought.

He thought of the apple trees he had passed the evening before, but thought, "I can't go hunting those trees at night somewhere along a fence row. I might get lost, and I can't risk walking outside the woods in broad daylight."

Hesitatingly, he walked on into the clearing. He saw no buildings or lighted windows anywhere. "Which way, God?"

he asked of the only One who knew where he was.

He almost yelled for joy when just ahead, in the light of the moon, he recognized potato stalks. "But these are not mine," he whispered to himself, remembering sermons he had heard about stealing. "They belong to some farmer."

His eyes glanced to the left, to the right, and straight ahead—a whole field of potatoes. How great! "This must be the answer to my prayer," he thought as he pulled out a still green stalk. His hands dug down into the dry soil and located five potatoes. He stuck some of them into his pockets and carrying the rest ran for camp. "Yeah, enough potatoes for a feast for several days," he thought.

Another thought struck him just before he left the bright moonlight to enter the woods. "I have no knife, nor pot to cook in, and even if I did, I have no matches. No nothing!" Defeat threatened his joy over finding food. Desperately, he tried to think how he could cook the potatoes.

"Tomorrow I'll think of some way to cook these potatoes." He promised himself. Then he thought of times he had seen his father eating raw potatoes. "That's what I'll do tonight," he decided. "I'll eat them raw."

Standing at the edge of the clearing outside the woods, Lester gazed up into the sky and saw the tiny stars twinkling in God's mansion. He felt so small and the pain of being unwanted by his mother caused a deep, almost physical, ache.

"More juice in a raw potato than a cooked one," he thought as he chewed and swallowed his first bite of the raw, unwashed, odd-tasting food. "Salt, pepper, and butter would certainly make this taste better," he decided.

Fear of getting sick warned him to go easy on a raw potato diet, but his hunger was so great he could not resist eating more. He munched down two potatoes.

It was night, but Lester had rested so much during the day that he was not sleepy. He sat on the ground and listened to the sweet music of the night insects. "Was it only a day ago I crawled down the porch post?" Lester asked himself. "It seems like a long time ago. But if God will provide potatoes for my food, living here alone is better than working for Frank. If only Shep was with me, I wouldn't mind staying here a long time."

Finally, as the eastern horizon grew light, Lester took another drink from the brook and crept into his hiding place urged on by the thought, "No way will I take a chance of Frank seeing me."

※◎※

Thunderstorms

Lester, accustomed to waking up at daybreak, found himself getting awake at that time no matter what time he had returned to his shelter during the night. His first thought as he opened his eyes and stretched his arms and legs was that Frank was not there to yell at him. Then he remembered there was no one but God and the birds and forest animals that even knew where he was or cared about him. The habit that would last a lifetime then sent him to his knees to say his daily morning prayers.

It was nice to quietly listen to the sounds around him and Lester soon became familiar with the morning songs of the birds. He wasn't used, however, to just lying around with nothing to do; he soon wished for some chores or just anything to break the monotony.

Nearly every morning, soon after whispering his prayers, he noticed a doe and her spotted fawn coming for their morning drink from the little brook. He tried to be their friend, but they did not approve of this strange creature. "This is like the Garden of Eden," he thought as he remembered pictures of all kinds of animals in the Bible story book back home. "The animals are not afraid of each other, but back then they wouldn't have been afraid of me either, so I guess it's different now."

One day as Lester awoke from a nap, he felt something crawling over his bare feet. A big, black snake, three-feet-long, was in his small hut. In an instant he was up on his feet screaming. Almost as quickly as he moved, the serpent was also out of sight slithering away through the bushes.

"Well, that's one creature I'd rather not have here." Lester said as he tried to calm himself by hunting for a big stick.

21

"All the animals I want for friends won't let me near them," he mourned. "The frogs that go 'burromp, burromp' at night always jump into the brook before I even see them."

"But I get so lonely," he grieved. "When it's foggy, I can go a little farther, but I don't want anybody to see me."

Worse than the snake was the thunderstorm that came up one afternoon a few days after Lester began living in the woods.

"We always went into the house when it stormed," he thought as he listened to rolling thunder and watched the trees sway in the wind. "Where can I go now?"

Storm clouds darkened the forest and the thunder cracked loudly. The tops of the trees swayed fiercely and the lightning flashed so bright that Lester could see deep into the dark woods. He jumped to his feet and ran outside the woods before he remembered someone might see him. He even wondered if he should run back to Franks.

"No! No! God will protect me," he thought. "He takes care of the other creatures here in the woods. They don't seem to be afraid, so why should I?" But he knew he was afraid and how he wished for someone to hold him close and protect him from the storm.

Suddenly, the rain came. He rushed into his shelter, but the roof was only leaves and branches, so he was soon soaking wet. The wind blew through his shelter and over his wet clothes. Chills shook his wet body.

Cradling his arms around himself, he tried to stay warm. Tears mingled with the streaks of rain streaming down his face and dripped from his nose and chin. He was afraid to move—almost afraid to breathe.

There was only one person to cry to, but his mind was so scared he couldn't find words to pray. Then almost automatically the words came, "Our Father which art in Heaven." He recited the whole prayer and as he said "Amen," he wondered, "Father, do you really care about me?"

His fears were over, and, confident that God would not harm him, he felt a calmness wash over him. He was able to again look around at what was happening in his small world.

He noticed a squirrel scampering up and down a tree nearby as if nothing unusual was going on. The brook was swelling with brown water, so he knew it had rained a lot and washed dirt off the fields.

He remembered how his father used to say, "A storm is God's way of speaking to people on earth and all should listen to His voice."

Lester shivered in his wet, cold clothes. The storm moved on and raindrops dripped from the trees as the small animals went about their daily lives. "I'm the only one who doesn't know what to do next," he thought.

A few streaks of sunshine glimmering through the trees in the west gave him an idea. "No one is out in such a storm," he reasoned. "I'll risk walking to the edge of the woods. The warm sunshine will feel good."

He thought of a bureau drawer in the house back along Heller's Church Road where he used to find dry clothes to put on. "Should I take off all my wet clothes, at once?" he wondered. "Maybe God wouldn't like that," he decided.

He took off his shirt and hung it over a branch to dry and then patiently stood in the warmth of the setting sun in the small clearing allowing it to dry his bib overalls.

"God is sending His sun to warm me," Lester said. "He still loves me. I can feel it—God's warm love."

The thunder still rumbled in the distance and he turned to watch the storm move away. "A rainbow, a beautiful rainbow," Lester whispered to himself and God. "I know it means a promise from God, but I can't remember the Bible story. When I get to church again, I must remember to find out about the rainbow," he promised himself.

The fear of a storm was almost forgotten when one night, a few weeks later another thunderstorm started brewing in the west. Lester had been running around outside the woods enjoying the night air and getting some exercise after a day of hiding and sleeping in his shelter.

First he noticed the lightning flashes far off below the horizon. He hoped the storm would bypass his woods, but before long a southeast storm moved in and over the woods.

The two storms seemed to concentrate their fury on the area where Lester stood, once again in rain-soaked clothes. He decided that this time he would not be scared. The other storm hadn't hurt him and his clothes would dry again when the sun came up.

Flash after flash lit up the woods and the thunder claps came on top of each other. Chills ran up Lester's back as he stood beside the trunk of a large chestnut tree. He heard the yipping of foxes, and, in the flashes of lightning, saw small animals running about.

As lightning and claps of thunder joined forces above him, a bolt hit somewhere nearby and Lester was thrown to the ground as the shock entered his body through his bare, wet feet. "OUCH! OW! OW!" yelled Lester frantically scrambling to his feet.

All thoughts of being brave left his mind and he was desperately afraid. The loud thunder was deafening—almost blocking his senses.

"OW, OW! Oh, please, God, where shall I go?" he cried with tears streaming from his eyes. Then as he felt another shock through his wet feet he started running out of the forest.

"Oh, please, please, please, God. I can't take anymore. What did I do wrong? Should I have stayed with Frank?" Suddenly, he wanted to say the Lord's Prayer again but was so scared he couldn't remember the words. God, however, knew and understood his unspoken thoughts.

Gradually the storms moved on, but Lester's fear still shook his body. "Please, God," he pleaded. "Don't let another thunderstorm come, for sure not at night and not like this."

Several more storms did happen that summer, but all were mild compared with that first night storm, so God answered Lester's prayer.

Alone in the Woods

Lester's nights and days were changed around. He slept part of the day, and at night roamed around exploring his unknown surroundings. It was usually hunger that aroused him from sleep, and he soon learned to tell the time of day by the position of the sun and the shadows of the trees.

He was forced to adjust quickly to living alone. He had no one to go to for advice nor had he any man-made tools to make life easy. His only possessions were on his back—underpants, shirt, and bib-overalls. No handkerchief, no comb, no watch, no knife, fork, or spoon. He also had no books to study to help fill long, lonely hours. He had lived in civilization for nine years and then suddenly was totally removed from all living persons and was forced to cope with life exposed to nature.

Now and then he wondered if it might be Sunday. He longed to attend church and again hear a Sunday morning church service. In his mind he reviewed some of the Bible stories he had heard in prior years. One was about the Garden of Eden and how Adam and Eve had eaten of the forbidden fruit. The punishment they received was to be cast out of that beautiful place.

He thought about the ten commandments and struggled with the one about stealing. He wanted to be obedient to what his father had taught him. "Never steal anything. Even though no one sees you, God can see you," his father had said.

"Well, if this is where God wants me to stay," reasoned Lester, "then God will also allow me to eat potatoes from the farmer's field. The birds eat what they can find on the ground or on trees. They do not starve. If I must live like the birds or wild animals, then surely I may eat of the farmer's raw potatoes."

With that idea settled in his mind once again, Lester would crawl out of his hideout and head for the potato field soon after dark. He noticed the wilted stalks drying on the ground and realized the farmer might see them and know that someone was stealing his potatoes. So, instead of pulling out more stalks, he dug into the sides of the rows with his bare hands until he found enough potatoes to fill his pockets again. He then carefully smoothed the dirt so nobody would notice it had been disturbed. After a careful look around, he dashed for the shelter of the woods.

Every night that Lester dug potatoes, even though he felt

God was leading him, he always asked God to forgive him for stealing. And always before eating his meal of raw food he said *grace*, as he had been taught at home.

He did not know which day in July he had left Frank's farm, but he knew the nights, when he roamed the woods, were cooler and filled with the sounds of the fall crickets' singing.

Summer was fading. The days he slept and sat alone in his leafy hideaway were getting shorter. The leaves and branches that formed the walls and roof were as dry as the dry leaves he had placed on the bare ground for his bed. When it rained, his leaf roof did not keep him dry.

Another Bible story came to his mind. The Children of Israel had tents to keep them dry. Also, every morning God provided manna for them outside their tents. All they had to do was gather it in baskets. It tasted like honey wafers and they lived on it for 40 years. Unlike Lester, they could gather their food in broad daylight and they didn't need to feel guilty about stealing it.

God also kept the clothes and shoes of the Children of Israel from wearing out. Nine-year-old Lester had no shoes and on cool autumn nights he shivered in his well-worn summer clothing as he went after his nightly food.

Taking a bath in the brook felt good in summer time, but the water ran cold as fall approached. With the hot, sticky days of summer gone, Lester bathed and washed his clothes less often. When he washed his clothes, he did the overalls first and hung them over branches to dry. He then put them on and washed his underpants and shirt.

Occasionally Lester walked cautiously to the edge of the woods hoping to see someone who was friendly, but only frisky rabbits and squirrels and the birds singing in the trees quenched his loneliness.

It was possibly two months before Lester heard the voice of another human being. Standing at the edge of the boundary which he had set for daylight hours, he heard shouting one day. Listening intensely he located the direction the sounds were coming from and soon saw a man and boy driving a wagon through a distant field. He was afraid it might be Frank and kept himself hidden.

His daily menu, for at least two months, was always the same—raw potatoes. He knew the birds had many choices of food, but they were free to hunt for it in the bright daylight hours. Lester had no salt or pepper to flavor his food and he craved for something sweet—maybe some honey. He prayed, "God, thank you for my food, but I wish for something else sometimes."

One cloudy night the little wanderer decided to explore further away from the woods. He hoped to find a field of corn in its early stage that could be eaten right from the ear. Finally, venturing beyond the potato patch, he discovered some other vegetables. He pulled up a stalk that, in the dark, looked like a red beet. Biting into it he realized it was a turnip. Something different! But raw turnips had no more flavor than raw potatoes. God had shown him a new food, and he then had two choices of vegetables. They at least satisfied the hunger of his growing body and he never became sick.

※✿※

Thanksgiving Morning

The rasping chatter of the locusts dwindled and the birds' songs were stilled. The branches of the trees grew more bare with each passing day, threatening to reveal Lester's hiding place. He had no way to prepare for the cold of winter but knew he could not live in his crude hideout much longer. The potatoes and turnips would soon be harvested or frozen. "If I freeze or starve to death, then God will take me to be with my dad," he thought.

Although he knew his mother did not want him and he had given up hope of ever seeing his family again, he was homesick. He longed to be a part of a family in a warm home. He needed more and warmer clothes and sometimes had to run through the woods to keep his body warm. His hair, which had not been cut since mid-June, was long enough to keep his head and ears warm. He had no mirror, but sometimes when he stared at his reflection in the water, as he stretched out to drink from the cool stream, he thought he really should have a comb and a haircut.

As the nights grew longer, his daily routine changed. He

slept part of the night, ate raw vegetables until his hunger was satisfied, but then was left with far too much time to think. When loneliness overcame him, he prayed to God — talking to the only Friend he had in his small world.

One morning he was suddenly aroused from sleep. Bang! Bang! Gunshots reverberated through the leafless trees. Bang! He heard voices. "God, help me! Is someone after me?"

He peeped through the drafty walls of his hideout. "Hunters! It must be November, the first day of small game hunting," he realized. "Oh, my! Will they see me?

"It wouldn't be so bad if it is someone who will love me and give me a home," he thought, "but surely the whole neighborhood knows about Frank's lost hired boy. They would make me go back!" So, burdened with fear, he stayed hidden all day.

Shortly thereafter the farmer dug all his potatoes, and Lester was left with only raw turnips to eat. He knew they wouldn't freeze until very cold weather.

A beautiful Indian summer arrived and for a few days the sun shone through the bare trees, bringing warmth and encouragement. The honking of wild geese filled the air, but as Lester watched their V-shaped formations flying south, fear of winter struck his young heart. He began to cry. "Only God knows where I am."

The nightly trips for turnips grew more uncomfortable as his bare, chilled feet stumbled over the frozen ground of the fields.

One morning he awoke earlier than usual, feeling wet and cold. Snow had fallen during the early morning hours and sifted through the drafty walls of his hideout.

He had known this would come sometime but had pushed the awful thought aside. Now the homeless nine-year-old boy knew he must find a home — somewhere to stay during the cold winter months.

Falling on his knees on the white snow-covered floor of his hideout, he prayed earnestly to God who had heard his prayers many times before. "God, have mercy on me," he cried. "I'm cold."

God said, "Run!"

He had heard the words once before—that night in the upstairs bedroom in Frank's house—"Run, run, run!" He was sure God had spoken to him again without using actual spoken words.

Shivering, he stood up and looked around. The shallow brook had a thin layer of ice on it. With a last glance of good-bye, he left his little hideout and started running. "God will lead," he said to himself.

Through the snow-covered fields his bare feet took him. He later figured he ran at least 20 miles before noon and has no memory of feeling tired or hungry during his flight. For the rest of his life he considered God had granted him a miracle.

On and on he ran through 20 miles of fresh-fallen snow. Around noontime he saw a house that looked a bit familiar. He remembered going to this house once when his dad had taken him on the trolley car a few years before. Something told him, "Here lives a friend of yours."

Timidly, he knocked on the front door. Cousin Lillie, a woman he loved dearly, opened the door and shouted in surprise, "Lester, is that you? You must be frozen, running barefoot in this snow. Come in, you poor soul. Where were you?"

The smell of cooking food almost overwhelmed him as Lillie told him it was Thanksgiving Day and that she had a chicken roasting in the oven. Taking the roast out of the wood-stove oven, she drew up a chair in front of its open door and said, "Here, Lester, sit here and put your cold feet in the oven."

She fussed over his soaking wet shirt and bib-overalls and brought a heavy blanket to cover him. "I'll run over to the neighbors and see if I can borrow some clothes for you."

She came back with an armful of clothes that the older neighbor boys had outgrown. Before long Lester was clothed in clean, dry clothes and sitting at the table eating a wonderfully good meal of roast chicken, cooked potatoes, and sweet, delicious pumpkin pie. How good it all tasted after four months of nothing but raw potatoes and turnips.

Between bites, Lester told Lillie and Chet Miller about his difficult summer and fall of 1922.

Lillie's questions ran together. "You're telling us you lived out there in those woods since July and had nothing to eat but raw potatoes and turnips? Those were the only clothes you had? Where did Frank live? In what area?"

"That's right," Lester answered. "I washed them in the tiny brook beside my leafy hideout. I don't know where Franks lived, but I overheard them talking about going to West Willow a few times. I was never allowed to go along when they went away. I had lots of work to do before they came home."

"Oh, you poor soul. Your sister told me you were hired out to someone. That's all I knew," said Lillie.

When Chet and Lillie told Lester he could stay with them, he thought it was almost like heaven to live among kind friends again. His days of living in the wilderness and eating manna (raw potatoes and turnips), which God had provided, were ended.

✳◉✳

Back to School

Cousin Lillie provided a good home for Lester and after giving him time to get rested, she decided that Lester should start school in January. Mary Snyder, the teacher at Lincoln School, thought he had been in school somewhere else for the beginning of the school term and asked to see his report card.

"I don't have any," Lester said.

"How come?" questioned the teacher.

Looking at the floor, he said quietly, "I was not in school since last March."

He was ashamed to tell his story of the past year and when he told Cousin Lillie about it that evening, she said she would go along to school the next day and explain the situation.

Mary Snyder was a wonderful teacher and she quickly learned to love Lester, the unwanted boy, dearly.

He in turn found learning easy and proved to be a good student, making excellent grades. Some schools held spelling contests with neighborhood schools, and when Mary discovered Lester's talent in spelling, she asked him to go with her to represent the Lincoln School.

The shy, little boy who had lived a secluded life in the woods for four months won the spelling bee. Winners often received a book as a prize and Lester could hardly believe that anyone would give him, a total stranger, a book—the first book he ever owned. He slowly realized he was living in a much different world from the one he existed in since the previous March.

On the way home to Lillie's house, the teacher also gave him a big bag of apples from her parents' orchard.

"Thank you, thank you, teacher, but I'm sure I don't deserve all this. Two presents in one evening." He felt overjoyed that people treated him so good and he could not resist doing something good in return.

He then revealed an unselfish and generous nature by giving his precious book back to her.

All throughout his long life, Lester treated people fairly, and God gave him the ability and the opportunity to do many good deeds for unfortunate folks. Matthew 5:7 says, "Blessed are the merciful: for they shall obtain mercy." Lester believed that and felt God would never allow him or anyone else to become poor because of helping the meek and feebleminded.

At Cousin Lillie's house in Ephrata, Lester had very little work to do after school in the evening. School lessons were easy for him. One day, near the end of the school term, he overheard someone mention that a farmer at Middle Creek was looking for a hired boy. The following Saturday he walked there and met the farmer, Joe Hurst.

Joe sensed that he was an energetic little boy. "How old are you?" he asked.

"Almost ten."

"How far do you live from here?"

"I don't know, somewhere in Ephrata."

"I'll be glad to have you work for me. How much must I pay you?"

"Nothing, I just want something to do," answered Lester, remembering the long days in the woods when he got so bored doing nothing. He felt happy just to work for his lodging if treated kindly.

Joe hitched his horse to the buggy and drove to Ephrata so Lester could pick up his clothes and the few possessions Lillie had given him. He cried for joy that evening while saying his prayers. Joe and his wife were treating him like their own son, the same as Christ Lapp and his wife had done.

The Hurst family showed their love to this willing worker by always giving him the easy jobs. They also bought Lester new shoes and a new Sunday suit which he wore every Sunday when he went to the Mennonite church services with them. He was thankful to be with people who would take him to hear the Word of God.

Threshing Wheat

Lester was at the Hurst home only a short time before they honored him with a nice birthday cake with ten candles. It was May 23, 1923, his tenth birthday. Remembering the harsh treatment of the year before, he thought, "I'll never run away from here."

The school term was over and he loved working for his new boss. It was great riding the horses during hay making. Although he was kept busy, it felt like fun compared to the scolding and punishment and going to bed without supper he had endured the prior year. "I wonder who is working for Frank," he thought. "Poor boy, whoever he is."

Six neighbor farmers helped each other during the July wheat harvest. The man who owned the threshing machine and tractor always hired some boys for the five or six weeks of the wheat harvest. Lester wanted to help, so he was put on the threshing machine platform to turn the sheaves the right direction to go into the feeder properly. He worked hard and the sweat ran down his face, causing the dust swirling up from the machinery to stick to him.

After a day working in the sultry heat of the dog days of summer, the threshing crew boys often cooled off and cleaned up with a good swim in a nearby stream. Often they slept out on the barn hill under the stars on a pile of newly thrashed straw.

Lester asked his boss, Joe, if he could sleep out with the older boys. He enjoyed sleeping out in the warm night air again, this time with pleasant companions and without the fear he had lived with the year before. Silently he praised God in his evening prayer for such a glorious life of sharing fun together.

When the Hursts' wheat was all threshed, the threshing boss said, "Lester, I would like to take you along with the crew every day. You do a good job."

"I would love to go, but you must ask Joe."

"Well," said Joe, "I know the young lad would enjoy it, but I feel it's too hard work for a ten-year-old." The next day, however, Joe asked Lester how he felt about the job.

"I want to go along. I don't mind working hard. I worked much harder last summer for Frank."

"If you want to go, go ahead and I will buy you a bicycle," promised Joe.

One Saturday afternoon when the threshing crew dropped Lester off at Hursts' at four o'clock, tired and ready for a bath, he spied a new, shiny red bicycle on the back porch. "I don't deserve such a wonderful gift," he thought to himself.

Then Joe came out and hugged him saying, "This is all your own."

"Whoopee!" yelled Lester. "I often wished for a bike, but didn't know how to get one. Thank you, thank you, Joe, for your kindness."

"Now," said Joe, "do you want to keep working with the threshing crew or stay here and work for me."

"I am so happy with the new bike that I want to help with the threshing until they are done." He felt God had richly rewarded him for doing his hard work properly.

Locating Mother

One Sunday afternoon after the threshing was over, Lester rode to Cousin Lillie's home on his new bicycle. "Praise God for Your goodness," he thought as he glided down a hill his hair flying in the warm afternoon sun.

"Hi, Lillie. I came to visit with you," he greeted his cousin upon arrival at her home. "I wanted to let you know how I like working for Joe."

After greetings were exchanged, Lillie exclaimed, "Oh Lester, where did you get that new bike? Is it really yours?"

"Yes, Joe Hurst bought it for me," said Lester with glowing face and joy in his voice. "Joe treats me like his own son."

A second reason for his visit was revealed when he asked, "Lillie, do you know anything about my mother or where she lives? What about Nathan and Florence? I haven't seen them for over a year, not since I went away last March."

Lillie had no information about the family but promised to ask around. When Lester ended his visit, he promised to return in a few weeks to find out if she had any information.

Several weeks later he rode back to Lillie's house again, and she was able to tell him that she had heard that his mother was working at McVey's Restaurant.

As he rode his bike to the restaurant, he wondered, "Will Mother be glad to see me again or will she not like me having a new bicycle and a good home?"

The owner of McVey's said, "Susanna is a dishwasher here, but she left for home already."

"Where does she live?"

"I don't know. Can't tell ya."

Lester felt confused about his mother. He was torn between a longing to see her and a fear of her reaction about him coming back into her life again. If he found her, would she send him away again to another strange place?

One night he asked God to help him find his mother again and that she would love him as well as she did Nathan. He ended his prayer as he often did, "Why did you take Father away from us? I need him here to love me."

The next morning when he woke up, he sensed God would lead him to his mother some day.

In late August Lester rode his bike to Lillie's home again. Her husband, Chet, had found out at work that Susanna Getz and her family were living in Lincoln, the town just west of Ephrata. He didn't know which house she lived in but described it and told Lester which street it was on.

Lester could hardly wait to see his mother, brother, and sister again, but it was with mixed feelings that he pedaled his bicycle slowly through the strange town looking for the house.

He found the street and finally was sure he had found the house. Hesitating on the sidewalk, he wondered, "Will Mother want me?"

All of a sudden Florence spied him on the sidewalk, yelled, "Lester," and ran out and hugged him. Her words tumbled over each other in a way that warmed Lester's heart. "Come on in. My, it's good to see you again. I thought I might never see my baby brother again."

Inside the door his brother's and mother's greetings lacked the warmth his sister had expressed. "Lester, how did you get here?"

Swallowing the disappointment of not getting a real mother welcome, he replied, "On my new bicycle. Joe Hurst bought it for me."

"What Joe Hurst? Where does he live?"

"How did you know where we live?"

"I found Cousin Lillie and she told me where you live."

Lots of questions were asked and answered, but his mother never mentioned Frank. Perhaps she felt guilty about what she had done. She did act friendly and Lester was glad for that. They talked for quite a long time and his family could hardly believe all he said.

"Do you want to stay here?" Susanna asked.

Nathan, his big, seventeen-year-old brother piped up, "He's not sleeping in my bed."

Lester's mother said, "You can sleep with me in my bed upstairs or on the couch behind the stove."

"A ten-year-old boy doesn't sleep with his mother," he thought. So he replied, "I need to talk with Joe Hurst first. See what he says."

He finally left the house with mixed feelings. He didn't want to push in where he wasn't wanted, but he didn't want to get pushed away again from his rightful home either.

✖☺✖

Moving Home

Lester rode his bicycle to school when it started again in September. He was in the fifth grade at Lincoln School and again Mary Snyder was his teacher. Although he felt she loved him better than his mother, he noticed she treated him the same as the other pupils. She treated everyone fairly and never created problems of jealousy by having certain pupils as teacher's pets.

While Lester was riding back to Joe's place one evening a few weeks after the beginning of school, a man from the newspaper office stopped him and said, "I see you have a good bicycle. We are looking for a boy your age to deliver the evening and Sunday papers. Would you be interested?"

"Sure, but I must ask my boss, Joe, first. He bought me this bike."

Lester discussed it with Joe who said, "You may take that job, but I want you to know that you may come back here for work anytime. You may live here or with your mother, whichever you prefer."

Lester decided to take the paperboy job. His wage of $1.15 per week was good money for a ten-year-old boy—especially a boy who had never had any money of his own.

Lester had another decision to make. He really wanted to live with his own family, but to live in the small, two-bedroom house might mean sharing a bed with his mother,

37

because Nathan refused to share his bedroom with his younger brother.

He considered his choices. The small, two-bedroom house was much better than his hideout made of branches in the woods. "At least I won't get wet when it rains," he thought.

He finally decided to move in. There was little privacy when the lights were still on in the house, so he had to undress in the shadow of the stove. He was almost as tall as his mother and was too embarrassed and ashamed to share a bed with her. Instead, he slept in the kitchen on the couch behind the stove. He was always glad when she got up at four o'clock to stir up the coal fire in the kitchen range and start breakfast of home-fries and eggs.

Susanna was employed in Lincoln, at that time, so after breakfast she kindled the fire down for the day and was off to work. After Nathan and Florence left for their jobs in Ephrata, Lester was able to lie down on the couch again until time for school.

During spring, summer, and fall, whenever the weather permitted, he slept on the rough floorboards on the back porch with only a light cover. That provided a bit more privacy, although he needed to dress and undress when it was dark.

Although his mother never once admitted she was sorry for having sent him away from home to work for a cruel man, she did accept him when she realized he was able to take care of himself and would not be a burden.

Another grief for Lester was that he craved attention, love, and acceptance from his big brother, but Nathan continued to show he didn't really want his younger brother around.

Every evening after school Lester went on his paper route. On Sunday mornings he delivered papers before going to church with Florence. He saved a part of his earnings in a pint jar which he hid in Florence's bedroom closet.

Spelling bee time arrived in the fall after the harvest was over. A good-sized crowd of spectators attended these evening affairs faithfully. Often teacher Mary Snyder took Lester, her best speller, along to compete against the best spellers of other schools.

The audience applauded and cheered when a student spelled a word correctly, and because he won so many spelling bees, Lester became well known. "Isn't that the boy who lived out in the woods a year ago?" someone would ask. "They tell me he lived on nothing but raw potatoes. His mom didn't want him."

Someone else was sure to say, "Smart little boy he is, even though he didn't go to school for almost a year. He deserves the prize. His dad was Sam Getz of Voganville years ago. Remember?"

"Sure I knew Sam. He was a fine guy. A hard-working man. Always honest," another would add.

Every time Lester received a book as the winner of one of the contests, he gave it to Mary Snyder, his teacher. She took the book to school where Lester and all the other pupils could read it. When she took him home in the evenings after contests, she always gave him a big bag of apples. Just as he shared his book with the pupils at school, he shared his apples with his family at home. He was kind and tenderhearted all his life, always sharing whatever he had with others.

Even though he had not attended school part of the previous year, fifth grade was too easy for him, so his teacher moved him on to sixth grade.

Each week the teacher called the classes to the front of the room to recite their lessons — reading, spelling, geography, and history. The method they used was called trapping. If a pupil did not spell a word correctly or give the right answer, the next one in line had a chance to say it. If the second pupil's answer was correct, he moved ahead of the other pupil. Every Monday the best scholars of every class were moved to the foot of the line. This way it was more fair and interesting for those who found it hard to learn.

By Tuesday afternoons, Lester was usually at the head of the class again. Every subject went easy for him. Some pupils lost interest in trying because Lester was always at the head of the line. Finally, the teacher moved him on to seventh grade. He was an excellent scholar and liked to help the slow learners. Also he never ridiculed them for mistakes. He played fair on the playground but showed little compassion if a person cheated.

❀

Planting a Garden

Lester was always looking for something to do. He liked to keep busy doing useful things. One day in early spring, when he was still ten years old, he looked over the good-sized lot that belonged to the property the family rented and got an idea. Before long he located a shovel and when he wasn't in school or running his daily paper route, he was digging up the sod.

The neighbors told him the lot hadn't been dug for years, and he had to work hard to accomplish anything. Although he usually tried to avoid thinking of the misery he had endured, he couldn't help but remember how he was forced to plow all day for Frank with the heavy walking plow. A feeling of relief and satisfaction surged through him. "This is lots easier, even if it is hard work," he thought. "I can rest whenever I'm tired."

Nathan showed no interest in anything Lester did and never offered to help with the garden project. Florence, however, encouraged him and helped sow lettuce and radish seeds and stick onions. When the subject of planting potatoes came up, Lester said, "At least I won't have to eat these raw."

"Surely not," laughed Florence. "I hope you will never need to live like that again, certainly not if I can help it. Didn't eating raw potatoes every day make you sick? Why didn't you look for some wild berries of some kind — huckleberries or blackberries — or even some wild honey? Surely there must have been some in the woods somewhere."

"Look, Florence, you don't understand." Lester answered seriously. "I was afraid of people after being at Frank's place. I didn't want anybody to see me and make me go back. I could satisfy myself with raw potatoes and turnips and I couldn't risk looking for things in broad daylight.

"I had no flashlight," he continued. "So I couldn't see in

the woods at night. I remembered how God provided manna for the Children of Israel everyday, and I felt He was providing me with potatoes every night."

Once started on the subject, he just had to ask Florence, "Another thing, why did Mother send me away? Did you know she was going to send me to live with Frank?"

"No, I didn't," she answered. "She would never even say where you were. She only told me, 'Don't worry; he's okay.' A few of the neighbors and also Christ Lapp asked about you and she told them, 'He's hired out to a farmer. You know he likes to be on a farm.' That's all she would say. I had no idea you were treated like that."

Lester turned eleven in May and kept himself busy hoeing, weeding, and watching his plants grow. He found it quite fascinating and wished he knew more. His mother knew about plants and gardening, but she took no interest in what he was doing. He tried to remember what Lavina Lapp had in her garden. "Peas!" he thought, but by then it was too late in the spring and they did not do well in the hot sun.

The family enjoyed Lester's radishes and lettuce and then he had another idea. "Florence, would it be okay to plant sweet corn in June yet?" he asked. "Dad used to grow it when we lived at Heller's Church."

"Oh, that would taste good. Sure, let me see if I can find some seed somewhere."

The corn was planted and the family watched it grow tall and full of ears. Lester was eager to share his bounty. The family enjoyed a few wonderful meals together, but only Florence really praised him for his hard work and for sharing the garden produce with them. His mother managed to say, "Tastes good." Nathan, however, ate his share without any comments or acknowledgment that it was a gift from Lester.

The garden, of course, didn't take all of Lester's time, so he worked for Joe Hurst again for several weeks that summer. He really enjoying helping again with the threshing, but because of his paper route every evening he couldn't stay and sleep out with the crew.

When the leaves fell that fall, Lester gathered enough

from the neighbors to cover the whole lot. He wanted a much larger garden the next year and had been told that leaves were good mulch.

Beginning in March and whenever the ground wasn't frozen, Lester worked to get his garden dug. Sometimes he was at it before going to school and again as soon as he was finished with the paper route. Sometimes he even worked after twilight by the light of the moon.

Finally, the garden was all dug and he worked hard with rake and hoe to make the dirt fine and suitable for planting. This took plenty of strength plus a lot of will power to keep at it.

He spent some of his paper-route earnings to buy seeds. Occasionally, Florence helped him plant the seeds and later hoe the weeds. During the summer and fall, his garden contributed to the family's meals many times. Often his generous heart caused him to also share his produce with a poor family across the street.

"I was 12 in May," he thought that summer. "Mother is 58 and doesn't earn much at her job. I need to help her somehow with her expenses." This was his goal and he saw it accomplished when his mother and Florence canned vegetables from his garden for winter.

Lester's muscles grew strong from all his hard work and at night he went to bed tired and with a feeling of deep satisfaction. He had many more things to be thankful for when saying his prayers than he had when he had prayed before spending part of a night sleeping on the ground in the woods.

He never missed saying, "Good night, Mother," and often his nightly prayers included, "Thank You, God, for bringing me here with my family. Tell Mother to love me."

His mother continued to show she loved Nathan more than Lester and he couldn't understand why. He wished his dad was still living. "We would be good friends," he often thought.

The Boys Need a Whipping

Lester's teacher had advanced him several grades in

school, so he would have started high school younger than most of the other students. Elementary school had recess, but in high school the pupils played sports. All the boys were ordered to wear tennis shoes, jockey pants, and a jockstrap. Lester said, "I can't afford to buy all that."

So instead of spending or borrowing money for sports, he went back to eighth grade for a second time. The school had double desks where two pupils sat beside each other in the double seat. His good teacher, Mary Snyder, was not at that school, and Lester soon found out that his new teacher, Myrtle, treated the pupils unfairly. She favored the girls in their lessons and didn't seem to care if they cheated. In fact, she would not punish them no matter what they did. Her treatment of the boys was quite different, and they lived in fear of her discipline. Often she banged their head down on the desk so hard that it created a big lump on their forehead. It sounded awful and hurt for a long time.

Each week the lessons included memorizing poetry. When a boy didn't have his memorization correct by the end of a week, he had to stay after school until he could recite the poem perfectly. Finally, after New Year's Day, Lester had enough of Myrtle's unfair treatment. He told the other boys, "It's not fair that we have to stay after school to say our poems. The girls get to wait until next week to say theirs.

"Hey, I'm going to put a stop to this," Lester said. "The next time she tells me to stay after school, I'm going to leave."

A few days later the eighth-grade boys were told to stay when the others were dismissed. Lester was the first one called on to say his poem. He said two verses then announced, "I'm not saying more. I'm going home. God created boys and girls equal and you should treat them the same."

"Who do you think is boss?" Myrtle asked. "You are not running this school, young man. You will do exactly as I say, now!" She grabbed her hickory stick from under her desk and marched down the aisle, biting her lips in anger with every intention of giving Lester a good whipping, but he ran out the door before she got to him.

Scott, another boy, said, "I'm going home too."

"You nasty brats, I'll teach you what's fair," said Myrtle. She ran after him but stayed close by the doorway to keep him from following Lester.

Scott jumped out a window and she screamed and swore angrily at the remaining boys.

Lester knew he had done something he shouldn't do, but he was laughing inside. The other boys ran around the room tormenting their teacher. Curiosity sent Lester back inside to see what was happening and she managed to give him a blow on his back with her stick. After that, he opened another window and jumped out too.

After the boys got out, they decided to go to Jack Fares' Restaurant for the rest of the day. Jack listened to their story about the teacher and invited them to eat there. He also encouraged them to do what was right.

That evening Myrtle called on Lester's mother to tell her about her son's disobedience.

Lester could hardly believe it when he heard his mother's reply. "I agree with Lester," she said. "You don't know how to teach big scholars. You won't have this problem if you treat everyone fairly."

"Does Mother love me after all?" he thought.

Myrtle, who despised men and made it clear she never wanted to marry, wasn't about to give in to the boys she also despised. "These two boys deserve a good whipping," she said. "I will not allow them to come back unless they get whipped by someone to teach them respect."

Lester decided to go see how things were going with Scott. There he learned that Scott's mother planned to take him to school the next morning so the teacher could whip him.

Curious to know how the teacher was going to whip a boy nearly as tall as herself, he sneaked up to a window and peeped in. Scott's mother, who wanted her son to receive a proper education and be able to move on to high school, was using all her strength to hold him over the back of a desk while a furious Myrtle whacked him again and again over his rear end.

Lester could hardly control himself from rushing in to rescue his screaming friend. He knew that when the beating was over, Scott would be bruised black and blue. "It's not right," thought Lester as he sadly went home for the day.

That evening a school board director came to see Lester. "Every day you are absent from school your mother will need to pay a fine."

Lester, who from his early childhood had been taught to judge all things according to the teachings of the church and Bible, explained the situation and what he had seen that morning. He finished by saying, "Our teacher does not teach with the love of God. She is evil and unfair to us pupils."

"I don't have money to pay a fine, and my son doesn't need to take a whipping," Susanna said.

"Yes," thought Lester. "My mother must have learned to love me a little. Maybe it happened when I helped supply food for the table from my vegetable garden." Throughout his life he felt that if he treated everyone kindly, they would become his friends sooner or later.

A few evenings later the director came again. "There is a school board meeting on Thursday evening at seven o'clock at John Shriener's house. You and your mother are to be there."

The school board members, the teacher, and Lester and his mother met at seven o'clock. Myrtle immediately spoke up, "Since I am the teacher, I have charge of everything tonight. This big boy is rebellious. He is making it hard for me to have order in school."

Lester tried to stay calm while she told lies about him. When he was asked to talk, he silently asked God what he should say. Then he said, "God created boys and girls, men and women, yellow, red, black, and white—all equal." Then he was silent. He thought about how Myrtle didn't mark his report card honestly, but he remained silent about it.

Again Myrtle stated more lies about him. She did not allow any other students or parents to be witnesses, so the board members, hearing only one side of the story, voted in her favor. They felt it was their duty to support the teacher, and not knowing about all her unfairness or how she mistreated the boys, they decided Lester should go back to school.

The teacher demandingly said, "With a whipping!"

The board members were in a predicament, so they decided to take another vote about a whipping. The vote was "yes." They hoped Lester would accept it.

Lester, however, thought about all the other innocent boys she would continue to treat unfairly. He was sure her unfair treatment would soon make others unruly and create more hatred toward her. He wished more witnesses of her teaching and discipline methods had been present to support the reason he had rebelled. He wondered if and how God would smite her for her wrongful acts sometime later in life.

In anger and frustration, Lester felt like crying. He didn't want to talk like this, but what came out was, "It's only fair that you hit first, then I hit with both fists, knock you down, and tear off your white cap."

The school board directors realized they had a big problem on their hands and were puzzled about how to handle the situation. They finally decided to expel him from school. So the outcome was that because of the school board's vote his school days were over. No fine was ever paid.

As Lester walked home with his mother that evening, she said, "Lester, tomorrow I'm going to tell Florence to stay home and teach you how to sew. Maybe if you have a little experience, you could get a job at a sewing factory."

That sounded good to Lester. Perhaps he could work and use some of his wages to help less fortunate folks.

Learning to Sew

Susanna knew by that time that Lester could do practically anything he tried or was told to do. She knew and couldn't accept it that he was smarter than Nathan. The harder Lester tried to gain her love by being obedient and sharing whatever he had, like the vegetables from his garden, the more she showed her preference for Nathan.

The morning following the school board meeting, Susanna said, "Your sister Florence will teach you how to sew with the sewing machine. Today you're to make a dress and apron for me. And do it right too! I'm not wearing any old rag-stitched dress."

Eager to please, Lester answered, "Yes, Mom, I'll do my best." But he was glad it wasn't his mother who was to teach him. Florence had always shown patience and kindness to her little brother. Now she instructed him and started him sewing on some old rags to get the knack of the old treadle machine. He thought it was great to try something mechanical.

At first, nervously biting his tongue, he rocked the treadle slowly. "This is fun," he thought as he watched Florence cut the cloth into pieces. Soon he was making straight seams and going faster.

He broke a few needles and Florence had to warn him, "You are not to sew so fast. You'll be fired the first day you work at a factory. Now go slow."

Eager to get started on real work, Lester demanded, "Where are the apron strings? I'm ready to make the apron."

"Lester, you are sewing too fast. I need to cut them first. Remember, Mother wants it done right. Don't be so hasty or you will make mistakes." Florence warned. "If you do, you will have to pick out the stitches and do it over again."

Soon he had finished the apron and Florence was busy cutting out pieces for the dress. "Mother will be proud of you," Florence said.

"It will be the first time she showed it, if she is," piped up Lester.

The dress was finished when Susanna came home. She smiled, but all she said was, "Lester." It seemed impossible for her to voice any praise for anything Lester did, but even though the dress didn't fit her properly, she wore it and the apron until they were worn out.

The next day was Saturday. Susanna wanted to rest and told Lester to iron the wash. He liked any kind of work and got right to the job.

During supper Susanna gave Lester orders, "Monday you're going to look for a job at a sewing factory. Tell them you can sew."

Nathan and Susanna both worked at Moyer's Knitting Mill and Lester thought it would be great to work at the same place, but his hopes were crushed when Nathan snapped, "Don't come in to Moyer's Knitting." It seemed as though Nathan could never bear to have his brother within sight.

Susanna said nothing to that outburst and Lester thought, "They really don't want me here. Nathan is still her pet; I'm just an unwanted boy."

✂◎✂

Working at the Sewing Factory

Early Monday morning Lester walked to Superior Shirt Factory in Ephrata. He went inside, found the boss, and asked about a job.

"How old are you?"

"Twelve."

"Can you sew on the sewing machine?"

"Yes, I made a dress and an apron for my mother on Friday."

"What does it look like?"

"Mom can wear the dress, it looks okay," said Lester, standing up as tall as he possibly could.

"How come you're not in school?" But then ignoring the

school situation, the boss said, "Tell ya what, this one lady isn't coming today, so there is a job available. Come with me."

He showed Lester how he wanted the work done and set him at the job of sewing buttonholes in shirts. Lester sent the needle flying up and down as his feet rocked the treadle as fast as possible. His tongue switched back and forth in his mouth, keeping time with the rhythm of the machine.

He didn't lose any time. Shirt after shirt was grabbed off the pile and soon ended up on the finished stack. Some of the women workers around him paused now and then to stretch and talk with each other. Lester, however, who was used to working under an unfair and harsh teacher, was ready to do an honest day's work and kept his sewing machine humming. He also did his work right. The boss examined it carefully and could hardly believe the quality and quantity from such a young boy. Often men did not qualify for this job. The buttonhole job was usually given to women sewers who had experience.

At the end of the day the boss discussed his wages with him. "We only pay $6 a week for 55 hours," he said. "Some of our best women are able to earn 30 or 40 cents a week extra as bonus."

The next week Lester's total paycheck was $8.10. This was a record. Lester was happy. He had earned several bonuses.

The following Monday a few of the women employees complained to the boss about Lester getting top wages. "He don't need such pay. He's just a boy; he has no family to support like we do. You did the wrong thing giving him that job and then praising him for his good work."

To keep peace among the workers, the boss changed Lester's job to sewing on buttons. One woman who was jealous of his pay and had complained that he had not been sewing right was given the buttonhole job, but she could not make the bonus Lester had earned.

Sewing on buttons was a tedious job. If the holes weren't perfectly lined up straight across from each other, the needle would hit the button instead of going through the hole. Lester's feet moved faster than his hands and pushed the treadle before he had the button in the proper position. Snap! The needle broke.

Frustrated, he changed the needle and thought about the woman who had taken away the job he had been able to do so well. "Are all women unfair like that?" he wondered. "Mom, Frank's wife, the school teacher?"

Determined to make a success of the new job, he got up his steam and thought, "I'm going to make as much money at this job as sewing buttonholes." He went at his work in earnest, but over and over he heard the snap of broken needles. To his frustrated mind, the noise each broken needle made sounded like a loud boom. He glanced around to see if anyone else had heard the noise. Sure enough, the lady who had complained about him was looking him straight in the eye. Snap went another needle. "Now I have to ask the boss for more needles," he thought.

"What's going on, buddy. You need to slow down. This gets expensive," the boss sputtered. Finally Lester was told, "That's enough needles for today. Better go home; maybe tomorrow it will go better."

Lester walked out of the sewing factory. "Maybe someday I'll go back again. I did like sewing buttonholes," he thought. "Well, God took care of me in the woods, so I will rely on Him to show me what He wants me to do.

Working at the Cigar Factory

Lester left the sewing factory at two o'clock and decided to try his luck at a cigar factory. He walked in and, not being sure what to do, roamed around and talked to a few of the employees.

Mr. Cressman, who ran that factory, soon came in with Mr. Bunty, a little man smoking a big cigar and manager of several factories. As he and several other men walked around, Mr. Cressman said, "I need another man in here."

Mr. Bunty asked, "What's that little boy doing in here? He's not working that I see. Hire him."

"Hey, young man, come here," called Mr. Cressman. He held out his hand and greeted Lester, "Glad to meet you. What's your name?"

Lester shook hands with a smile. "Name is Lester Getz. I'm out of work."

"I'm the boss of this place," Mr. Cressman said. "How about working here?"

"Sure. I'll do a good job," said Lester, hoping nothing would be mentioned about school. "I like to work."

"Could you start right now?" asked Mr. Bunty.

"Sure," said Lester. "That way I'll get a good start and know what to do tomorrow morning."

Mr. Bunty motioned to an old man. "Mr. Leisey, this is your new man or boy, I should say. Get an apron for him and show him what to do."

Soon Lester was wearing a waterproof apron and standing in front of a tub of water. Mr. Leisey gave him the following instructions: "This is where you work. Put a box of tobacco beside you, take a handful of leaves and dip them in the tub of water. When they are wet, put them in the box on this other side. When that box is full, set it back along side the rest of those boxes and go get another box of dry tobacco."

Lester's hands flew from box to tub to box on the other side. He could work as fast as he wanted to without a worry of buttons being straight or needles snapping. The work around him was all hand work and without the noise of running machinery he could talk with the men working not far away. "This is fun," he thought. "Well maybe it will get boring some days."

The first time he took home a full week's pay it was $12 cash. The family could hardly believe it. Nathan and Florence earned $6 a week each, and Susanna earned $7. From their earnings, the three oldest members of the family put $4 in the kit each week to help pay household expenses. Lester, although he was the youngest, donated $5 a week. Most of the rest of his wages went into a jar—his bank for many years.

Years later, during the Depression year of 1930, when Lester was 17 years old, the cigar factory began laying men off from work. Someone, however, always needed to work a few hours every Sunday turning the sweat boxes. The boss did not want to work on Sunday, so he asked Lester if he would be willing to do the work.

Lester gave the answer of a mature person. "I will not miss church services on account of tobacco," he said. "But, if no one else will come, I will work a few hours before the services. What time may I start?"

"What time do you prefer?" asked Mr. Bunty.

"If I could work from five o'clock until seven, I can still get home and take a bath before church services," said Lester. "Is that okay?"

"That would be fine. I trust you. Just keep the doors locked," Mr. Bunty answered. "Now don't you tell anyone, but I'll pay you $2 for those two hours." (Sunday workers always got $2 for a half day.)

"Sure won't tell," promised Lester.

In the fall of 1931 Lester was the only worker left. Finally, the factory closed. A lot of men were out of a job during those hard days of the Great Depression.

Butchering the Turkey

Lester had to stay busy. The folks in Lincoln soon recognized the fourteen-year-old boy who rode his bicycle through town. They also discovered he was willing to do whatever type of job he was asked to do.

Kit Diem liked to go to card parties but didn't like to drive alone at night. Sometimes a few other women went along, but Kit felt more secure having a man along, so she asked Lester to accompany her. He liked to play Hoss and Peffer.

Contests were held at the card parties twice a year. The prize was usually a turkey and for seven years Lester won prizes. One year a big live goose was awarded to the winner and Lester won that also. A turkey or goose was a worthwhile prize for poor folks, especially those who had no work.

The first time Lester brought home a live turkey, he was quite proud of it. He put it down in the cellar for the night where no stray dog or thief could get it.

As the family was eating breakfast at daybreak the next morning, the turkey woke up too and flew at the cellar window trying to get out and creating a racket.

"What's that?" asked Florence excited about the noise under her feet.

"My turkey," shouted Lester. "I won it last night. Will you help me butcher it for Christmas? We'll have a real feast for all of us."

Lester built a small pen for the turkey beside the barn. He bought corn to feed it and watched it grow bigger.

"Hey, Sis, when are we gonna kill the turkey?" inquired Lester one evening at supper. "How about tomorrow? Suit you?"

"Yeah, but you'll have to kill it. That's your job," she declared.

Neither Susanna nor Nathan offered to help with the project, but they were curious enough to watch out the kitchen window. Nathan, who never wished any good for his brother, hoped the 20-pound turkey would flap his big wings and whack Lester really hard. He even felt it would be great to see Lester's prize get away from him. The hard feelings were one-sided. Contrary to the treatment he received, Lester remembered how generous his dad had been and following that example shared the good things that came his way with the whole family.

Killing the turkey turned into a big project. The family owned neither ax nor hatchet, so Lester and Florence carried the turkey to the wash line and tied it there with both legs tightly bound. Lester next approached with a butcher knife in one hand and grabbed the turkey's head with the other hand. His face and hands were spattered with blood by the time the head was cut off, and then the big, headless bird flapped wildly.

"It worked," Lester shouted to his sister with glee. "Now let's pluck the feathers."

Lester knew the neighbor man across the street had no job and had five children to feed. He remembered how good a meal of cooked meat would have tasted to him when he had lived alone in the woods. He also remembered how his father had taken bags of candy to the neighbor children at Christmas, and so, when the turkey was roasted on Christmas day, he said, "Those children across the street are probably hungry. I'm going to take them some turkey."

Mother and Nathan didn't approve of him giving the food away, but Lester took a good portion to the neighbors anyway. He was an unselfish boy and received a hearty "Thank you and God bless you," from the neighbor family.

Lester Trips on a Stumbling Block

The cigar factory was not a good place for fifteen-year-old Lester to work. He worked with a group of men and boys all older than himself. Some of the guys were rough and rowdy and used foul language and alcohol. They laughed at Lester when he refused their treats of free drinks at the hotels. They called him a sissy. "Never hurt you," they would say.

Even though times were hard, they spent nearly all of their pay on drinking and gambling. Wives waited at home alone and children went to bed hungry while the husbands and fathers wasted the little money they earned.

Lester knew drinking was a bad habit. He was determined to not give in to their coaxing and taunts even though he was the only one to refuse.

Daily he heard cursing and swearing all around him and then one day he realized he was using the same bad words. He knew it was wrong, but because he had never given his life over to the Lord, the devil was able to trick him into stumbling into this sin. His tongue found it easy to use the words his ears heard over and over again.

His working comrades continued to tempt him to join them when they drank after work and evenings at hotels.

"I'll just drink a little to get them off my back," he thought.

The devil, however, is never satisfied with a little. The evil men made bets with Lester over who could drink the most. Before long Lester liked to drink and could drink a lot of whiskey in one evening. In that cunning way, the sin of drink overpowered Lester.

As the evil habits of cursing and drinking increased, his ambition to work fast slowed down. Through betting and spending time with the wrong type of men, he was well on the road to becoming a true alcoholic. He knew that what he was doing was not right, but he liked being one of the gang.

When he was alone, however, he felt ashamed. His guilty conscience bothered him and he asked God for assistance. "God, I need your help," he pleaded one evening at bedtime. "Help me break away from this evil sin. I'm giving all my money to the devil. I don't want to live like this."

At work the next day he heard the same cursing and God's name being used in an evil way. He thought he could keep quiet and let them have their fun, but when payday came, the gang planned a great evening at the hotel again.

Trying to stay true to his decision to not drink any more, Lester said, "Nope, I'm not going."

They scoffed at him and because he was trying to be good on his own power, he soon agreed to go along. The evil one had won another victory.

The gang told him later that he had drank more whiskey than ever before. He didn't remember much of the night and was too drunk to walk. He did remember crawling on his hands and knees through the snow into a parked car somewhere. He woke up at five o'clock the next morning cold and wet from crawling in the snow. He felt miserable. "This is it," he said. "No more. I'll never see Dad in heaven if I don't change."

By asking God to take control of his life, he won the victory and was able to quit. Never again in his lifetime could he drink beer or whiskey. He often wished that year could be erased from his life and his memory, but he knew that God had forgiven him.

Two months later Nathan had to have an abscessed tooth pulled. Having a decayed tooth extracted was a very unpleasant thing. For Nathan it was even worse than usual and he experienced a great deal of intense pain as the dentist struggled to get the tooth out. Somehow the dentist broke his jaw.

Infections from the abscessed tooth and broken jaw caused Nathan to get very sick, and a doctor had to be called one night. He stayed until two o'clock in the morning and then confessed defeat. "I can't do anymore," he stated. "I think you should get a pastor."

Lester, the brother who could have remembered the many times that Nathan was unkind and had failed to help him, hurried to a restaurant to use the phone. All calls went through a switchboard at the telephone exchange and the operator told Lester the pastor he asked for wasn't at home.

Desperately, Lester said, "Call another pastor."

"You must tell me who," the operator replied.

Almost crying, Lester said, "I don't know another pastor. Call yours."

The operator reached E. M. Rhodes, the United Brethren pastor, who promised to be at the house within an hour.

When the pastor arrived, Susanna, Florence, and Lester stood beside him at Nathan's bed. He prayed that God would take the awful pain away and make Nathan well. Then he asked, "Do you wish to be baptized and be a church member?"

Lester, always soft-hearted and wanting to make it easy for Nathan, pleaded, "If you want to accept Jesus as your Savior, I will go with you to church when you are feeling better again."

Nathan nodded his head, "Yes." He was too weak and sick to talk.

After he was well again, the brothers were baptized and joined the church in the spring of 1929. Lester was 16 years old.

Life Goes On

The Great Depression affected people in all walks of life—those who lived in cities, towns, and villages. People grew discouraged as their jobs disappeared and they were unable to support and provide for their families.

Those who lived on farms and those who had space to have gardens were able to grow vegetables and did not suffer from lack of food as much as those who had to purchase all their food.

Lester also experienced problems during that period of time and grew quite discouraged. He spent more hours working in his garden and was able to provide food for his mother, brother, and sister after they lost their jobs and had no income.

There was a time when Lester was the only one in the family who had a job, so they were dependent on his income to pay the rent and other bills.

When the cigar factory closed in 1931, Lester was glad to get away from the workers who mocked and tempted him every day. Even so, some of them continued to ask him for money whenever they met him. They always promised to pay him back, but knowing their habits he was sure he would never be repaid.

"Come on," they begged, "don't you trust us? Can't you lend us a couple of dollars?"

"No," Lester replied many times, "I know your money goes to buy drink at the bars and I won't help you satisfy that habit. If you are hungry I'll share the produce from my garden, but I'll not give you money."

He found a job doing piecework at Eby's Shoe Factory, but many days he ran out of work and was sent home early. Even with taking care of the garden he loved, he still had time on his hands. "I better not loaf around or I'll get into mischief," he thought, so because of his skill and reputation as a good worker, he was able to find another part-time job at the Ephrata Shoe Factory.

There was a time that Lester had to ride the trolley to get to work, and after paying his board and trolley fare he was left with only $1.57 a week for all other expenses.

Lester was now an adult and felt it was fitting that he live in a place of his own. He rented a small two-room house for $6.00 a month.

A good friend, Henry Hummer, asked him if he had the money to furnish his small home.

"No," Lester had to reply. "I have very little money."

"We've always been good friends," Henry said, "go to Eitmer and Hoffman Furniture Store and get what you need and bring me the bill. I will pay it and you can pay me whatever you can each month. I'll never charge you one cent interest."

Henry also offered him a nice combination stove. The part that used coal would provide heat for the little house in winter and could be used for cooking. During the summer when the weather was too warm to want extra heat in the house an attachment provided electricity for cooking. Lester accepted the stove and it worked fine.

Lester didn't want to run up a big debt so he bought only what he considered necessary—a bedroom suite with spring and mattress, a kitchen table and four chairs, plus a day bed for what he called his living room. His food was always the plainest and cheapest. He lived in that small house for four years.

The house had no bathroom, so while living there he shared an outside toilet behind the house with nine other people. No appointment was needed to use the toilet and the neighbors all got along well. Rather inadequate ventilation was provided by quarter-moon designs cut in both sides of the privy. Everyone knew the use of a small building with that design cut in the door or sides.

It was during that period of time that a new shoe factory

started up. Lester was asked to be the manager of the shoe-sole department at double the wages he was getting at Eby's Shoe Factory. Eleven months later the company went bankrupt and Ephrata Shoe bought it. Lester's promise of double-wages proved of no value when the job disappeared. He had a good reputation at Eby's so he went back there again.

Lester, who had only six and a half years of schooling, proved himself a brilliant and valuable employee wherever he worked. He wasn't working at a place long before he could run all the machinery.

Because folks went barefoot a lot of the time in summer, work in the shoe factories was usually slow during the warm months. Shoes could, however, be taken to Eby's for repair work and that provided some work in slack times.

The Denver hat factory offered Lester a summer job. Knowing men with families needed steady income, he accepted the job so employees at Eby's could work more hours. Once again he took advantage of an opportunity to help others.

✳❦✳

A New Car

In 1937 Lester decided to buy a new car. He wanted to pay for it with cash and to do so he needed to earn more money. The Eby's Shoe Factory was busy and he was working long hours, but he also looked for a part-time evening job.

Mr. Gerth from Wernersville offered him a part-time job selling memorials (tombstones). He gave Lester brochures with pictures of the different kinds he would sell.

"I'm not a salesman," Lester said. "I can't sell them."

"Yes, you can," replied Mr. Gerth. "This will make the extra cash for you. Try it."

Lester advertised in a few papers and, to his surprise, his sales were good.

He put the money into the jar he kept hidden in the cellar. Months later the jar was almost full of his commissions from selling memorials and what money he could save out of his wages at Eby's.

One Saturday he drove his old car to the Ford dealer. Under the seat was the jar of saved money. A new, 1937 two-door sedan caught his eye. Since he seldom hauled passengers, he didn't need a big car.

"What's the price?" asked Lester.

"Six hundred thirty-eight dollars."

"Hmmm!" Lester mumbled. "Well, I have only $630 in my jar. I'll have to wait until later. Hope it won't be sold."

"That's okay," the dealer said. "Pay the rest later."

"No, I don't charge anything. I like to pay as I go."

A few weeks later Lester returned and purchased the new car. He sold the old one soon afterward.

✺

Drafted for War

After working at Eby's Shoe Factory for nearly 11 years, Lester decided to work for Armstrong in aircraft manufacturing.

In 1942 the United States was involved in World War II, so there were many jobs available building airplanes and other things connected with the war. He did not want to fight in the war or kill anyone, and he hoped the war-related work would help to keep him from being drafted into the army or navy.

A few weeks later the manager of the plant said, "You are liable to be called to the army. Do you want a deferment from active duty to stay here at the aircraft factory?"

"Well. I sure don't want to go to the battlefront, because I know I can't shoot anyone. I just can't!" said Lester. "But, maybe if I ask for a deferment some man who is a father with children will need to go."

He knew lots of men who enlisted and others who were drafted to go to war. Since any man under 35 was subject to the draft and he was only 28 years old, he felt sure he would soon receive his draft papers.

He wondered if God would provide a way so that he wouldn't have to go kill people. "Can I rely on You?" he prayed.

That evening when he came home from work, he found

a deferment card that had arrived in the mail that day. The next day he told his boss about it.

The boss reassigned him to work in the department that repaired aircraft. They needed reliable help—people they could depend on every day.

About a year later he got draft papers again. He took and passed the physical examination and got all the shots servicemen needed. A week later the United States Selective Service law changed—no man over 27 years of age was to be drafted. He was called to fight and had been close to going, but apparently God had other work for him.

"I have a new job for you," his boss at Armstrong said. "We need to hire more people and a lot will be women. Do you think you can teach women?"

"If they are willing to learn, I should be able to teach them in three days," said Lester.

Lester stayed at Armstrong until the war was over.

Sunday School

Many states had laws that forbid businesses from operating on Sundays and parts of the Pennsylvania Blue Laws were in effect until around 1970.

Lester was busy everyday except Sunday—that was going-to-church day. He earned a metal pin for 13 years of perfect attendance in Sunday school.

"I need someone to help with opening devotions for adult classes," Lester's Sunday school superintendent said. "Can I depend on you?"

"Yes," smiled Lester. "I am willing to work for the Lord. You can count on me."

He was also asked to help on the Visitation Committee. In that church anyone who was absent from church services three Sundays in succession received a friendly visit inquiring about the absence.

The Sunday school superintendent also asked Lester if he would help him hand out tracts in his spare time on weekday evenings. When he agreed, the two men stood outside the doors of a hotel and gave out tracts, hoping to convert people from their drinking habits.

One day Lester saw some tracts in a book store. They were about the evil habits of drinking and gambling and he liked the way they presented the message.

He showed them to the Sunday school superintendent who asked, "Who are you going to give them to?"

"I intend to give some to my Sunday school classes and also ask them to distribute some to others. Too many men are spending their money for drink and the little children hardly have enough clothes to wear when it's cold. Surely God wouldn't object to me handing out these tracts, would He?" asked Lester.

"It's best to only give them to people who voluntarily accept them," the superintendent said. "Don't force them on people. Some alcoholics might get mad. We don't want anyone to get hurt. Salvation is each person's choice."

A New Trade

Lester wanted to start a business of his own and upon the advice of Libby Star, a hairdresser, he took a course in beauty culture at Bryland Institute in Reading. He thought hair dressing might be a good business without a large investment.

He completed his course of training in five weeks and got a job in Reading with Edna Rose. He drove back and forth between Ephrata and Reading five days a week, but the cost of gas was more than he felt he could afford.

He wasn't sure if it was proper for him to be working with women's hair every day, but decided to walk a straight path and avoid allowing any woman to become more than just a customer. From the beginning he was careful to treat each lady the same.

After Lester had been working with Edna Rose for two months, she bought new equipment for her shop and offered to sell the old equipment to him at a reasonable price. He bought it and moved it to his home in Ephrata where he opened his own beauty shop.

He figured if he did a good job, he would have business

as long as there were women around. His rates were less expensive than some shops and because he did good work, his business grew—much faster than he expected. Some women who were used to his work in Reading came to his shop in Ephrata as long as he dressed hair.

❦

Bartending

Business was slow when Lester first opened his beauty shop. One day a customer offered him a part-time job. She suggested he work part-time for her until his business provided full-time work.

"What is that?" asked Lester.

"Bartending five nights a week from ten o'clock until two in the morning."

"Huh," snorted Lester. "No way, I don't drink, never mixed any drinks. I drank some as a teenager, but I often wished those years would never have been."

"I would teach you," she said. "Think it over until next Thursday when I come for my next appointment."

After she was gone, he called his Sunday school superintendent and told him about the job he was offered.

"Now look," was the unexpected reply, "take the job and hand out those tracts to anybody that will accept them. God has opened the door for you in a mysterious way that you would never have thought of."

Once again Lester remembered how, when he was only seven years old, his father had said, "What God tells you to do, you must do." So although he felt guilty as a Sunday school helper to be working in a bar, he decided he was being asked by God to help convert alcoholics.

When the lady came back for her next appointment, she asked him again about taking the job. He showed her the tracts and said, "If I work for you, I will hand these out to every customer."

"Fine," she agreed, thinking he wouldn't do it long. "Soon you'll have lots of friends. Some of the fellows will want to buy you a drink. Since you don't want to drink, take their money and use it to buy more tracts."

He sensed what she was thinking, but he was determined it wouldn't happen. He knew he needed support from God to help him stay true to his decision to never drink again.

The next Monday night Lester entered the bar. The lady showed him how to serve beer, wine, and whiskey and how to mix drinks. He hated the smell of liquor and he hated the foul language he heard there.

At closing time his boss made her first attempt to get Lester to drink. "We always have a nightcap together before we go home," she said. He gave her what she asked for and filled a red wine glass with water for himself. They sat together at a table and while she drank her liquor he drank his water.

Night after night Lester passed out his tracts. Some men looked at them and laughed. Others stuck them in their shirt pocket. Some made fun of him and called him a goody-goody. They told him he wouldn't last long in there.

By the second week he knew some of the fellows and decided to walk with them going home. He talked about Jesus and hoped they would feel guilty about wasting their money and time in the bar. Some confessed they knew better but could not break away from the habit. They told him about drinking away their weekly wages and having to live a ramshackle life of misery with broken marriages and unhappy children. He encouraged them to quit and some did. Others remained addicted for many years and spent all their money and were unable to ever own a home.

"It's not worth it," Lester would plead. "Read these tracts. Go to church. I broke away from that habit when I was only fifteen. It can be done. You must pray for help."

Occasionally he took men home in his car, because they were not fit to drive their own cars. Often their wives were up waiting for them and when he had to help the men into the house, he often noticed the women had been crying. He gave the wives tracts also, saying, "Show it to him every morning." They usually thanked him for trying to convert the husband.

He kept buying and giving out tracts. He noticed some

men were not coming to the bar as regularly anymore and some not at all. "They may be going to another hotel," he thought, but he had a feeling they wanted to quit. He never used any pressure on anyone, and many of the men actually got to like him.

His boss continued to ask him to drink with her before going home. She figured she was getting him to like it, but starting the second week Lester mixed a little water with her whiskey and continued having his glass of water. The third week he reduced her drink with more water and again sat drinking his water. Apparently she had little taste left after years of drinking, because she didn't detect what he was doing, but he was gradually getting her away from alcohol.

The fourth week Lester mixed his boss a glass of half liquor and half water. By the end of the fifth week she was drinking only water. She didn't want to believe it when he told her what she was drinking, but she had to. Her plan had not worked as she intended.

She told Lester, "I saw how your beauty shop business was growing and I thought by hiring you for awhile my liquor sales would increase and I would reap a big profit through you. Instead, my business decreased. Some guys who have been coming here for years have quit. But I must admit, you only did what you told me you would do."

"I asked the Lord to help me. I trusted that He would," said Lester. "He has helped me since I was a little, eight-year-old boy." Then he told her of some hardships he had gone through. She was amazed but believed him.

He pleaded with her to go to church. One Sunday he helped 14 people through the sinner's prayer—the bartender lady was one of them. Some of those people were baptized and joined the church. The bar was closed and the bar sign taken down. A while later a restaurant sign was put up.

Meantime, Lester's hair dressing business grew and provided plenty of work. He did good work and to accommodate his customers, he opened at five o'clock in the morning so women could stop for appointments on their way to work.

Mother's Death

Lester's mother, Susanna, lived with Florence in her old age. He visited her occasionally, but she rarely asked him anything—about his job or his life. He still felt he was her unwanted son.

The last six months of her life she hardly spoke to anyone. She ate very little food and drank only a little water.

A few months before her death, as Lester was standing at her bedside, she took his hand and said in a very feeble voice, "Lester, will you take care of Nathan after I am gone?"

With tears running down his cheeks, he answered, "Yes, Mother."

He had sought her love until the end, but it seemed as though she still rejected him as a son—there was no place in her heart for him. He did not want to judge her, so he put his hurt in God's hands. He was 31 years old when she died.

A Homeless Family

One warm summer evening in 1947, a customer came running into Lester's beauty shop saying, "My daughter needs help. I know you help anyone if at all possible."

"I'm busy until eight o'clock," answered Lester. "Come back after closing time. We can talk then."

At eight o'clock she returned with her daughter and explained that her daughter and the daughter's husband and two children had lived in a double house. The landlord's daughter got married and he wanted that part of the house for her.

"When my daughter came home from work," Lester's customer said, "the children were sitting on the porch crying. The door was locked and a note tacked on the door read, 'Your furniture has been moved to the barn.'"

Kindhearted Lester said, "I'll try to help these folks in their predicament. I have an extra room and a sofa."

The customer's daughter said, "I only need one bed. My husband generally works nights and my two girls can sleep at my in-laws' house on Saturday and Sunday nights when he is home. We'll make out."

"I'm not going to separate this family," Lester said. He figured that the girls could sleep with their mother the nights their father worked and sleep on the sofa on weekends.

The family was always grateful for Lester's kindness. They stayed at his house until they found another place a few months later. He treated them like a father would and charged no rent.

Remodeling House

Many evenings Lester worked until after eight o'clock in his beauty shop, hardly taking time off to eat. He couldn't say no to his customers, but eventually he lost interest in the work—he grew tired of seeing hair all day. Some ladies wanted new styles and were hard to please. He didn't want to hire help or buy more equipment and eventually it caught up with him. He had a nervous breakdown and closed his business.

Occasionally he became dissatisfied with his lonely life. Sunday afternoons, when he wasn't busy working, he sat alone in his rented house and cried and prayed for strength to go on. "If mother didn't want me, why was I ever born," he thought. He realized it was depression that brought such thoughts and that he should not think such things.

Lester had noticed the friendly employees of Cloister Dairy as they went from door to door delivering milk. He applied for a job and was given a route. Then he was asked to be foreman and work a route whenever someone wanted a day off. He was not satisfied with that job and asked to have his former route back again. They wanted him as foreman, but Lester minded the stress that went with that job. So he quit.

He next went to work at a furniture store as a part-time salesman for Beauty-Rest® mattresses.

God had given him the ability or talent to enjoy work and to do it well. When faced with problems—from schoolwork to repairing airplanes to remodeling a house—he was able to find the right solutions and work them out properly and quickly.

He had been saving his money and after paying rent for many years he decided to buy a house of his own. The house he could afford needed a lot of work. With his know-how, he was able to do most of the remodeling himself. "This is a challenge," he thought as with pick and shovel he dug the cellar deeper. The dirt he removed needed to be carried up the steps in a bucket. The next job was just as hard. He had to mix the concrete outside with a hoe and shovel, put it into buckets, carry it down the steps, and pour it to make a floor.

He tore out the old coal bin and installed an oil tank under the front porch. He put a new roof on the house, a new chimney was erected, and he had an oil heating system installed in the cellar.

The outside toilet was taken away and replaced with a new inside bathroom. All this remodeling was hard work and costly. It took over a year to complete, but finally it was finished right down to new carpets and linoleum. Looking at the nice house gave Lester a good feeling and satisfaction of a job well done, but the nice house didn't bring him the one thing he longed for most—the companionship of a wife who loved him.

Lester hoped to find a good Christian woman with whom he could serve the great God who had kept and protected him all his life. He knew he could trust God and so he continued to pray for a good, spiritual wife.

He knew from experience that God does not always answer prayers immediately so he did not lose faith. Therefore, waiting for an answer kept him going to the Lord more earnestly.

Although it was hard work, he had thoroughly enjoyed the challenges he had faced in the remodeling of the house. Since he was working full time at his regular jobs during the day, the remodeling work had to be done mornings and evenings before and after work.

Besides the paying jobs Lester held, he was often asked to counsel and work with alcoholics. He felt God wanted him to do this. When calls came for help, he couldn't refuse because he knew little children suffer when their fathers or mothers are drunkards. Although he did not think his mother had been an alcoholic, he well remembered the rejection he had felt when she was too busy to pay any attention to him or refused to show him love.

Being called on at any time of day or night created an irregular schedule and this also caused stress in his life. He sometimes wished he could say he was not available to go out when called. On the other hand, he didn't want people to get hurt because he didn't do what he felt God had called him to do.

After many prayers he sensed God had assured him that

he would someday have a good life here on earth, and that he should keep on showing kindness and helping others.

That assurance gave him strength to keep on working with sinners who wanted to break away from the bad habit of drinking.

Selling Beauty-Rest® Mattresses

Lester was a well-liked salesman. Folks talked about the salesman who gave good deals and treated his customers honestly. He made some telephone sales of the Beauty-Rest® mattresses in his spare time and didn't hesitate to drive quite a distance if he felt he could make a mattress sale. He also still sold memorials part-time.

His boss at the furniture store recognized Lester was bringing money into the business and offered him bonuses for every mattress he sold. He kept handing in orders and told his boss, "Keep my bonus money until November. Then I want to use it to buy Christmas gifts for my neighbors, friends, and some children."

Before long his boss told him that he was one of five top salesmen from eastern Pennsylvania, New Jersey, Delaware, and eastern Maryland being awarded paid vacations. "You are higher in sales than anyone else here," his boss said. "You can pick one of our other salesmen to go with you."

Lester picked his good friend Dave. Their first dinner was at Housners Restaurant in Baltimore, Maryland. Both ordered seafood platters. Thinking he would have a high-priced meal for a change, Lester ordered a lobster dinner. The man sitting next to Lester at the counter had ordered fried night crawlers (probably shrimp).

Dave said, "How can you bear to sit next to those worms? Ugh, I can't eat."

Lester looked at the creature on his plate. "Well, I must taste it for sure. Might be better than it looks," he said as he cracked it open. He picked out some meat, dipped it in fried butter and chewed and chewed and chewed.

"Come on, Les," said Dave. "I can't eat with such ugly food on your plate."

71

"No more of this stuff," Lester said, and the men got up and stomped out the door laughing. They decided there had to be better places to eat and perhaps rich, expensive food wasn't that great after all.

All in all, they had a good vacation paid for by the boss. They enjoyed three fine meals a day, but saw a lot of food going to waste and into the garbage pail.

"I'll never forget this," Lester said. "It's not right how folks order more food than they can eat."

"I should have just asked to have the money added to my bonuses," he decided. "I would have had more pleasure buying Christmas gifts for other people than working so hard to have fun taking this vacation."

As they drove homeward, Lester's thoughts focused on a problem he knew he would face and wished he knew how to resolve it.

Losing His Home

Through some unwise actions and decisions, Lester found himself in a situation that caused him to lose his house and car and most of his personal property. A person he had thought was a friend had betrayed his trust and demanded almost everything he owned.

He had tried to be kind and not take advantage of others, but this person had taken advantage of him. He could have proved he was right, but he didn't. In spite of hurt and anger, he chose to release his right to the things he had worked so hard to buy.

God had helped him before and he was sure God would help him again. "You have not forsaken me," he told God in prayer, "but why are the people you created so difficult to live with and why do they hate each other so often?"

"It was easier living alone in the woods," he grumbled to himself as he packed a few bags with his clothing and prepared to start his life all over again. Then God reminded him of his hunger for good food and the loneliness he experienced when he had not even one person to talk with for four long months.

Once more he walked away from the only home he had. He felt as grieved and hurt as he had been as an eight-year-old child. Even his mind felt bruised by the betrayal of trust he had placed in his friend.

His thoughts went back over the many, many things that had happened in his life before. He had always tried to be kind and had tried to treat everyone with respect, but this was the outcome.

Lonely and without money, he trudged to Good's Hotel. Briefly he explained his situation and said, "I need a room, but I have no money to pay you until payday."

The owner trusted Lester and told him it was okay to pay the rent whenever he had money to spare. He showed him one of his cheapest rooms—seven feet wide and nine feet long. A little metal wardrobe stood beside the narrow window and the single bed took up so much of the rest of the room that he had to get on the bed to pull out the dresser drawers. The place had one bathroom shared by 19 renters. Lester learned that the only way to avoid a rush to use the bathroom was to get up at five o'clock in the morning.

He sat alone in his tiny room and remembered the other time he had been all alone—the months he had spent in the woods. He wondered if he would ever have a happy life on this earth. "God, You delivered me out of that place in the woods," he prayed that evening. "Will You help me find something to eat this week?"

In spite of all his sadness and discouragement, he decided to put his trust in God to help him again. He had only enough change in his pocket to buy a loaf of bread. "Should I go hunting for potatoes again at night?" he wondered to himself.

Friends would probably have given him money to see him through the week, but he didn't want to discuss his situation with anyone. Without a car or money for bus or trolley fare, he started early and walked to work the next morning. Already his stomach was reminding him that a meal had been missed.

All day he tried to think of a way to remedy his food problem. Once when he stood looking out a window, he saw a lot of plantain leaves on the lawn. He knew pigs liked to eat them and because of that people often called them pig-ears. (Common plantain is considered a weed. It has broad, flat leaves and is richer than spinach in iron and vitamins A and C.)

At quitting time Lester walked to a store. He visited there with other customers and then bought one loaf of bread. That left him with only four cents in his pocket. Upon leaving the store he walked the streets until it was dark and then went back to the place he worked and pulled off a lot of the pig-ear leaves. He stuffed them into his pockets and returned to the hotel where he washed the leaves at the wash basin in the shared bathroom. A refrigerator was available for the use of the people who rented rooms and he stored his precious food there after making himself a pig-ear sandwich. For four days, until payday, he lived on pig-ear sandwiches and didn't have to borrow money from anyone.

Lester stayed at the hotel a few months until he had enough money to pay for better lodging. He decided to keep all the bonus money since starting all over again was very hard. He needed to skimp on every necessity so he could afford to buy a cheap car as soon as possible. At least he had several jobs. He continued to sell memorials and mattresses by telephone in the evenings, and he also volunteered to work with alcoholics whenever the police called him in on a case.

❧

Working with Alcoholics

Lester had gotten involved with the drinking habit as a teenager. He had seen the sin of the habit and, with the help of God, had broken away from it. His strong advice: "Never start it, then you won't ever need to quit it." He wished the state would outlaw all beer joints.

People who are involved with drinking and getting drunk often encourage their friends to join them. Young people and old alike find themselves involved in this evil habit which breaks up homes and causes much pain in families. When the devil gets a person trapped in alcoholism, their lives are wrecked and their money wasted. Without help from the Lord or a person to counsel and help them, there is no hope for a good life.

Sometimes Lester received a donation for his work with alcoholics, but usually it was volunteer work. He always asked God to help him know how to approach the problems. He worked hard to help folks, especially to avoid family breakups, and although he had no official position, he was God's servant right where he lived and worked. Nasty remarks were often shouted at him, but he was able to accept them without anger. Many of those same people became his friends later in their life. Knowing he had helped save a person from alcoholism was all the reward he needed.

When people refused to listen to his advice, he got discouraged, but then the words of his kind father would come back to encourage him, "What God tells you to do, you must do."

He seldom heard God speak in an audible voice, but through prayer and his conscience he knew God was leading him to help others.

One of the cases the police referred to Lester involved a fifteen-year-old boy. The evening before, a bartender had noticed the teenager was getting out of control due to drinking too much. The bartender called the police and they called Lester.

Lester went to the lockup to talk with the boy. "What happened?" he asked.

It took a lot of talking, patience, and pleading, but finally the boy confessed he drank too much and then didn't know what he was doing. He did remember he had broken a table.

Lester was quite aware of how things went in bar rooms, but he went to the bar to get their side of the story. "Did you sell liquor to a minor?" he asked. "You know that is forbidden by law in the state of Pennsylvania. You are at fault to begin with," Lester scolded.

"As long as the boy has money, I'll sell him drinks," argued the bartender. "Who are you to come in here telling me what to do?"

Not knowing that Lester was working with the police, the bartender continued, "Here, let's have a drink together."

Lester indignantly told the bartender that he should have taken the boy home to his parents and told them their boy was doing wrong. "Instead," Lester said, "you got him into trouble just to make money. Shame on you! Do your own boys drink in here too or do they drink at some other bar, knocking down tables? You are violating the law and making extra work for the police. You either quit selling liquor to young boys or this bar will be closed."

The bartender laughed and said, "Mighty big talk you have."

Upon Lester's report and advice, the police closed the bar and padlocked the door for 30 days. After the padlock was off, the bar was reopened for business.

Before long he got another call from the police. A man had been arrested the night before and was in jail. Lester went to the same bar again to inquire about the man.

"He broke a window last night, " the bartender said. "He got drunk and then got mad. Nearly busted the door down." Then as though he had nothing to do with serving the drinks, he added, "Some of these guys don't know when they have enough."

"Why don't you keep track how much each person drinks?" said Lester. "If you controlled that, you wouldn't have damage to your property. Besides, you are ruining lives and families. You are stealing their hard-earned money."

"No. Nah," replied the bartender. "I need the money. I gotta make a living too. I need all the sales I can get."

"It's a bad way to make a living," remarked Lester. "My, oh my, God does not approve of your work."

As Lester left the bar, he met Dan Fry, a carpenter, and asked him to fix the door and window.

"Eight dollars for the job," said Dan.

It wasn't Lester's duty to pay for the damage, but to show the bartender he wanted to do good to all people, he paid the bill.

When he visited the prison again, he saw a few more young boys. He asked their names and ages. One was 15 and one was 16. He got them to sign a paper stating they drank at that bar every Saturday night. Their confession showed the police that the bartender was still selling drinks to under-aged boys.

The bartender was arrested and the bar closed for another 30 days. It never opened again.

Rutt's Furniture

Lester, because he had lost his home and needed to start all over in life, needed to save money for his unknown future. Although he didn't know how it might happen, he still felt

God would give him a nice home life again some day. Dave, the friend he had taken along on his vacation in Maryland, left the furniture store and got a job at Rutt's Furniture.

A college graduate was hired to replace Dave. He was to unpack and move furniture and help Lester with sales. Lester soon noticed the college boy preferred to stand by the door waiting for customers rather than doing the harder jobs. He also noticed that the college education didn't seem to help sell furniture.

Once when Lester asked him to help in the work department, the young man replied, "Well, sir, don't you know I am a college graduate? I don't do work like that."

Lester didn't like his attitude and said, "Buddy, you'll never amount to much just standing around waiting for sales to come your way. Hard work never hurts anyone as long as he is healthy."

Lester told his boss, "Either get rid of that young man or I will quit."

The young man was not fired, so Lester left the business and went to Rutt's Furniture and was again working with Dave.

⚜

Recognizing Another Stumbling Block

During trials and heartaches a person has two choices. He can rely on God as his strong support, or he can allow the devil to persuade him that he deserves better things. While it is good to have fun, a person must be sure it is clean fun and doesn't hinder anyone from being a Christian.

While Lester was working at Rutt's, he became friends with a group of men who were also employed there. Compared to Lester, they were a wild bunch. One of the things they did was to go bowling every Friday night at Blue Ball Lanes. After some coaxing, Lester allowed himself to be persuaded to go along and became a part of the group.

Soon after, one fellow said he knew where an old army parachute was for sale. Well, Rutt's had a small plane and an idea was born! The men went together and bought the parachute. The next Sunday morning they went to the New

Holland airfield and practiced jumping from the airplane.

This was great fun and they decided to jump every Sunday morning at 7 a.m. A lot of folks were attracted and came to the field to watch. Before long the crowd of curious people got too big to control safely. The men decided to start two hours earlier to eliminate such a huge crowd, but the audience also came early.

Quite a few of the onlookers and participants missed church services to attend the jumps, and Lester was one of them. He knew it was not right and sometimes left before his buddies were done with this sport so he could attend services. He enjoyed the fun and the companionship of the men but knew he was dishonoring his Master.

Even though his father had died when he was only eight years old, he still influenced Lester's life. "Dad would never have missed church services for any kind of sports," he thought. "Why am I doing this? No more! This is it," and he quit attending the event. Eventually the men were ordered to stop jumping on Sundays.

Saving a Business

After Lester had worked at Rutt's Furniture for a year, his former furniture store boss called him one day and invited him to lunch at Yorktown Hotel in York, Pennsylvania. He wanted Lester to come back to work for him at his Ephrata store. The store's record for the past year showed the business was deep in debt. "We're not having enough sales," the man said. "I want you to be manager of the store."

"I don't want to be a bookkeeper," replied Lester. "I want to sell."

The man offered him good wages and Lester promised to work for one year if he had permission to reduce the prices of the furniture as he saw fit. "It's in your hands," was the reply. "Bring my sales back again. I've lost too many customers this past year."

One day the store manager said, "Clean house; there're too many items here that people don't want. Reduce the price tag. I am tired of looking at it in the display room."

Lester reduced the price tags down to one-fourth of their original selling price.

The manager said, "We can't afford to sell furniture for such low prices."

"It's better than having it sitting here for six months," answered Lester. "Be fair to customers and don't try to rip them off. If your prices are too high, people will shop somewhere else.

"You are trying to get rich quick," Lester continued. "Do honest business and, believe me, Mister, you will make a profit. That's the way it works."

The reduced items sold within a week. Old customers returned and new customers started coming to the store.

Each month items that had stood on the floor for nearly a year were reduced and sold. As he saw his profits increase, the manger thanked Lester for teaching him a better way of doing business. He had learned the hard way.

Lester did any job he was asked to do, some more interesting than others. He liked getting out among other people and sometimes he was asked to help deliver furniture. That involved some heavy lifting, getting big pieces of furniture through narrow doorways, and walking backwards down the hallways. He had to be careful to pace his footsteps to the other delivery man's and most of all avoid putting any scratches on walls or furniture.

Sometimes when they delivered a piece of furniture, they found no one at home and faced locked doors. If the weather was nice, they sometimes set the furniture on an open porch, but some folks complained if it was not put in the room where they wanted it.

One day they came to a house and found no one around. They spotted an open upstairs window. Lester crawled up a porch post and swung his forty-year-old body up on the roof. "These windows are locked," he said, "and I can't reach that open window from here."

"Hey, I've got an idea," said Bob, the truck driver. "I'll get this wash-line prop and you set your rear end on it and I'll boost you across the three feet from the porch roof to the open window. Grab the window sill and go for it."

"Okay, I'll try, but don't you let me fall."

"Here we go," said Bob.

Lester grabbed for the sill and pulled himself across while Bob pushed and laughed. It was a struggle to get a good grip, but he finally tumbled into the room along with the screen. "I made it!" he yelled.

In seconds he was downstairs unlocking the door.

Lester tried hard to look on the bright side of life even though his life had many hardships and also heartaches. Seldom did he complain to his fellow workers, but every morning and evening he shared his sorrows with God and committed himself totally to His care.

Facing a Man with a Gun

One day Lester got a call at work from a man. The man said, "Come right away. A fellow just went into a house in a mad rage and he has a gun. I'm sure he'll shoot the woman who lives there." He then gave an address and hung up.

Lester knew where the house was and who lived there. "Oh, Lord, help me," he said as he fell on his knees. "What should I do in this situation? Why don't they call the police?"

As he prayed he felt God was asking him, "Would you lay down your own life for someone?"

Lester was the only employee working in the store that day and at that moment there were no customers. He locked the doors, got into his car, drove down the street. As he drove he asked God to spare his life and also that of the lady who was in danger. He felt God's call to rescue friends, relatives, and even his enemies and sensed God was with him.

"Will I lay down my life for someone?" he questioned. "Yes, I must do God's will," he decided.

He parked two houses away from where he thought the trouble was.

Dutch Sweigart, a policeman, was standing at the corner of the next house. He waved his hat slightly to get Lester's attention, and speaking in a low tone said, "Don't go in there. The man has a gun. You're liable to get hurt. Wait until more help comes."

Lester never carried a weapon of any kind, but out of his memory came Bible characters who had won victories. David, the little shepherd boy, would not go out to battle the nine-foot-tall Goliath wearing armor. "Neither will I," declared Lester to himself.

Walking cautiously along the side of the house, he approached the back porch. Gene Tuffy, another policeman, was standing guard there behind a boxwood shrub. When he saw Lester, he didn't dare speak loud for fear the fellow inside the house would hear and get more disturbed, so he just shook his head urgently.

"Don't go in," he whispered. "He has a gun and I saw him load it."

Lester did not heed the policeman's command, but went up on the porch, opened the door, and walked inside—right past the man with the gun. He was receiving courage from the unseen hand of God and was not afraid.

The man cursed Lester and asked, "What are you doing in here?"

With the bravery of God to support him, Lester stepped over to the man and asked, "What are you doing in here with a gun in your hand, buddy?"

Lester got a hold of the man's hand which held the weapon and pointed the barrel right into his own belly and said, "If you want to shoot, shoot now."

The woman standing directly across the room by the window screamed when she heard Lester say, "Shoot now." She did not have the faith of God that he had.

The man seemed confused and became even more emotional as he faced Lester, a stranger who showed no fear of his gun. He shook all over and couldn't talk.

Lester took the gun from the man's hand without any hassle. He unloaded it and put the shells in his pocket. He also asked for any extra bullets the man might have. In a daze the man reached into his pocket and gave them to Lester. This was almost certainly the first time in his life that anyone calmed him down in such a way.

Lester said, "I'm taking the gun with me. You won't need it again, I don't think."

Lester had learned to deal with violent people by not showing fear, and by trusting his safety to the Lord. He was sure God had saved him throughout his life for *such a time as this*.

Lester walked out the front door with the weapon. Dutch walked up to meet him saying, "Feel my back; I'm all wet from sweating. I was sure you would get killed in there. I don't see how you got that gun from him." He talked about Lester's braveness for many years.

Lester put the gun in the trunk of his car and left.

Never Refuse the Work of the Lord

Another incident occurred one Saturday. The boss asked Lester if he had any objection if he left work early to meet his in-laws in the afternoon.

Lester said, "It's okay with me as there are hardly any customers coming today in all this rain." So at noon the boss left.

The rain continued and no more customers did come in. After completing some desk work, he checked the lights on all three floors and at five o'clock locked the doors, and left for his apartment.

His car was at the garage for repairs so he walked home in the downpour and dropped off a deposit at the bank. By the time he got home, he was soaking wet. He was so miserably cold and wet that he even decided to do without his evening meal at the diner—the snacks he kept in his apartment and often took along to work for his lunch would have to do for supper.

He took a bath and shaved but even after he was in dry clothes, he still felt cold so he snuggled under the covers in his bed to get warm. "I'd rather be warm than getting wet just to eat a good meal tonight," he thought.

At such times Lester found himself longing for companionship. It would have helped his loneliness if Nathan had been a brother with whom he could share things. His life, however centered around his work, his friends, and his church and Sunday school. He never felt close enough, however, to any of his friends to share his deepest thoughts and burdens. A good loving wife would have been nice, but as it was, God was still the only One he talked to about his loneliness.

At nine o'clock as he lay on his bed listening to the radio, the phone rang. Someone said, "You better come right away.

I saw a man go into a house threatening to shoot the woman who lives there"

"What's the problem?" asked Lester anxiously. "Who are you?"

He listened as the man explained and then said, "Call the police. My car is at the garage for brake repairs and I'm not coming out in this heavy rain."

"I thought I'd call you to save time because they often call you anyway," the man said.

Lester told him he had not even gone out for supper because of the weather and hoped that was enough to convince him to let him alone.

Immediately after he hung up Lester became jittery and could not relax. He thought of his motto, *Never refuse the work of the Lord*. "But this is a policeman's job. They are being paid for their work," he argued with himself.

Feeling guilty about refusing to help someone in trouble, he decided, "Well, I can at least pray for the woman." Out of bed and down on his knees he prayed that God would not allow the man to harm the woman. A quiet, inner voice said, "It is someone you must save."

Lester continued to excuse himself by explaining to God about the heavy rain and that he was too tired to go out again that night. "Besides all that," he reasoned, "I don't have a car and haven't eaten a full meal all day."

Suddenly a loud, shrill voice right beside him said, "It is someone you must save!" The light was on in his small room and Lester could plainly see that no one else was there.

All doubts and hesitation were gone as he answered, "Yes, God, I'm on my way."

Quickly he got on his feet and dressed. He ran down the hall and took the steps two at a time.

Outside the door he fumbled to open his umbrella, but the wind was blowing so hard it turned the umbrella inside out before he had crossed the street. He ran close to the store buildings, trying to avoid some of the driving rain, but he was soon soaked. The town seemed deserted and he saw no one else on the streets.

As he ran, he thought how Jesus had given up His own life to save others. He remembered the other time he had faced a man with a gun and had felt God was asking him if he was willing to give up his life for someone.

"I will do my best," he decided, "even if I get hurt. Jesus was not a coward; neither will I be."

When he got to the right street he had to guess which house was the one with the trouble. "This is probably it," he exclaimed to himself as he saw a house with lights on the first floor.

As he went up the steps, the door opened before he touched its knob, and Lester entered the room. A man with a revolver was right inside the door cursing a woman who was standing by a window.

The man was acting as though he would shoot her or anyone who got in his way.

Then Lester understood why God had sent him. Outside the window a wide-eyed youth was standing right in line with the woman. If the man aimed for the woman and missed he could very easily shoot the boy outside.

Lester remembered that God had said, "It's someone you must save," but it wasn't until years later that he found out what the plans were that God had for that youth. As he faced the man, however, he only knew he had been called and could rely on God's help to save the youth even if it cost him his own life.

He did the same as he had done before. He took the man's hand which held the gun, placed the barrel against his own stomach, and said, "Now shoot." The trigger wasn't pulled and Lester took the gun away from him without any more trouble.

He mentioned to the man about how his life would have changed if he had taken a life. How he almost certainly would have had to serve a life sentence in jail and surely would never have forgotten what he had done. "That one second of anger would have changed your whole life," Lester counseled. "You better thank God that he sent me here in this pouring rain. Very easily I could have stayed home. God has something better for you in life than to sit in jail. You were working for the devil."

The man soon left the house with what Lester hoped was a look of shame on his face.

"How did you get in the house?" the woman asked Lester. "Did you have a key? I know the door was locked."

"No, I had no keys," said Lester. "I didn't need any. God must have opened the door, because it opened before I even touched it."

"Who does this gun belong to?"

"I don't know," the woman answered.

"Well, where did the man get it?" inquired Lester. "It looks like a new gun and I doubt that man had money to buy a new gun. I think you better check and see if you can find a receipt."

The woman thanked him for saving her life and that of the youth outside the window and added, "Oh, I was so nervous and scared I just prayed and prayed someone would come to stop him."

Lester then told her and the youth who had come into the house how a loud, shrill voice in his room had told him, "It is someone you must save." He added, "If you didn't believe in prayers being answered before this, I hope you do from now on. I don't think you'll forget this night."

"God needs both of you yet," he said. Then turning to the boy he added, "Don't forget, sonny, prayer saved your life."

Things had happened so fast that Lester had forgotten the weather, but he shivered as he went back out into the driving rain in his still wet clothes carrying the gun. "I hope no one sees me," he thought. "If they do, they are sure to think I am up to something."

Back at his apartment he hid the gun in a closet and shed his wet clothes. As he changed into a warm, dry robe, he thought about what had happened and thanked God that he had heeded His call. He also asked forgiveness for not responding immediately.

The woman found a receipt that showed a $5 deposit had been paid for the gun and two bullets. The balance of the bill was due sometime later. She brought it to Lester and it made Lester angry that anyone would sell a gun to an angry man. "Someone is going to hear about this," he promised himself as he noticed the name of the store on the receipt.

Monday morning Lester left his hotel and discovered Dutch, the policeman, waiting to discuss the situation with him. He asked Lester for the gun, but Lester replied, "I am taking the gun back to where it was bought and they better give back the $5 deposit. Too many businesses are selling their products just to make money. They are working for the devil when they do that.

"If someone didn't have more than $5 it showed he was an irresponsible person and not fit to own a weapon. A business will make more money if run in an honest way. Do you believe that?" he probed.

"Yes, I guess you are right," grunted Dutch.

During lunch hour Lester went to his room and got the gun and the two bullets. At the shop, he laid them on the counter and said, "I am bringing this gun back. Someone who should never have owned a gun bought it in here last week with a $5 deposit. You can have the weapon, but I want that money back."

"Yes, well," stammered the owner of the store trying to think of a way to make more money out of the deal. "I will need $10 to clean it up again so it will look like new again. How do you know he bought it here?"

"I have the receipt from this shop right here. You have no right to sell guns to angry people. You know people don't approve to it. If someone had been hurt, you would be responsible and no doubt have a big fine to pay," said Lester. "Furthermore, don't you know it pays off three-fold to do honest business?"

The owner was not willing to return the deposit and came around the counter to get the gun from Lester.

Lester's temper got the best of him and he held the gun up in the air out of the man's reach and then threw it down on the floor as hard as he could. He grabbed the owner by the throat and put him up against the wall.

Just then Dutch walked in and said, "Lester, let him down. I'll take care of this." He then ordered the man to give the $5 deposit to Lester.

Lester took his hands off of the man and the money was handed over. As Lester hurried out the door, he thought, "I was overpowered by a spirit and not the Holy One who helped me all my life. I know I'm often tempted just the same as anyone else, and I'm not perfect. I have to be strong and do what is right. God helped me many times and if I do what is right, God will reward me hereafter."

Later that evening he called and told the woman to come and get the $5.

Marriage

While Lester was working at a furniture store, a lady came in to buy a stereo. Lester watched as she walked around looking at the furniture and appliances. Something about her appealed to him.

She bought a stereo and liked it so well that she told her friends about the store and how pleased she was with the stereo. Later, her friends came in to make purchases also and they talked to Lester about their friend Betty who had recommended the place.

Lester, hoping to establish a friendship with Betty, called her on the phone and thanked her for the sale she had helped him make. As he had hoped, the phone call led into friendship and dating.

Lester was careful to learn if this woman was a true Christian lady. He knew the answer to that question when she invited him to attend Sunday school and church with her. They were soon attending church together every week.

Their friendship and trust grew and Lester and Betty were married on June 30, 1968, at Coleman's Memorial Church by Rev. Etter. They had a wedding picture taken in the rose garden by the church. A reception was held at a restaurant in Sinking Spring.

Betty treated Lester with respect and kindness. She wanted to make her husband happy.

Finally, Lester was a happy man living with a good wife in a clean, well-kept house. "Thank You, God, for a home and a Christian wife who loves me," he often prayed when he thought of Betty. "It was hard to go through those times when my mother didn't want me, Frank treated me so rough, my brother showed how much he didn't like me, and my friend caused me to lose my home. I guess I might have been impatient through those trials if I had known the good things You had in store for me."

He was no longer an unwanted person driven from his childhood home and later from the house he had remodeled. The sorrow and sadness of those trials was replaced with the joy of living with Betty, a true Christian companion. "I'm sure this is a marriage that will last 'til death," he often thought. Life seemed filled to the brim with good things.

He remembered the good days when, as a child, he had worked at Christ Lapp's and Joe Hurst's farms, but the memory that his mother did not love him always created a sad feeling. Never in his life could he understand the reason why his mother rejected the little, innocent child he had been.

Several years after he and his wife were married, he won a contest at his place of employment. The prize was a free vacation to Barbados in the Caribbean Islands. It was snowing the January day in 1972 when Lester and Betty flew out from a New York airport. It was 71° when they arrived in beautiful, sunshiny Barbados. They had a wonderful vacation.

On May 2, 1973, Lester and Betty had a little boy they named Samuel Oliver: Samuel after Lester's father, and Oliver after Betty's father. Their joy, however, turned to grief when the same day he was born the good Lord chose to take the little one to that beautiful home on high.

With aching hearts, they thought about their child who was gone. Knowing he was safe in the arms of Jesus helped a great deal, but they couldn't help but wonder why God had taken their child. They had already loved him and had planned to care for him and teach him about the true God.

"Little Samuel Oliver will never have to live alone as I did," said Lester as he and Betty discussed their grief. That thought made it a bit easier for Lester to give him up into the care of God.

"He was such a wanted child," Betty said as she mourned for her son. "Oh, how could any mother ever give away her own son? But, if Jesus wants him in heaven, we willingly want to accept it." All their lives they loved him and thought of him being with the angels in heaven.

Heaven seemed closer and a bit more real after Lester and Betty buried their little baby. The experience did not make them give up their faith or think there was no use living useful lives, being honest, or helping people in need.

※◈※

End of a Job

One day Lester sold an electric range to customers at the furniture store. After it was set up, they discovered they got an electric shock whenever the burners were turned on.

Lester was sent to check it out for faulty wiring. He recommended the stove be exchanged for another range since it had never worked properly.

Instead of agreeing with Lester, an electrician was sent to fix it, but he could not get it to work right either.

Lester insisted a new range be sent to these folks, but the boss said, "We'll need $120 more for it."

"No, sir, that's not right" stormed Lester. "Their stove did not work the first day they had it. This one here in the store is the same model as the one they bought and I'm sending it out and see that it works properly."

They loaded up the other range and after it was hooked up, it worked perfectly.

He hated to say it, but he had to, "The boss says your bill is $120 more for the exchange and hookup."

The folks were not happy with the deal, and, after talking a bit, Lester marked their receipt paid and went back to the warehouse where he unloaded the faulty range and went to the office. There he handed the receipted bill to the boss and pulled $120 from his own wallet. "I'm paying this out of my own pocket," he said. "I can't work for you any longer. I won't work for a firm that asks me to do dishonest deals like this.

"It's not right," he continued. "I don't believe in stealing at night and no one is going to pay me to steal in broad daylight like this deal was." He then threw the keys on the desk and walked out the door, disgusted but unemployed.

※◈※

Working at Gimbels

Meanwhile, Gimbels was getting ready to open a store

at Park City, a shopping mall north of Lancaster. Lester applied for a job and explained to the head manager about what had happened at his last job.

"Hey, you're just the type of guy we're looking for—an honest man," said the manager. "We are opening up for business in two weeks, but you can start today by getting things set up in the carpet department."

Deep down Lester wondered, "Did God have this planned? Every time I stand up for what is right, even if I lose my job, I get another one right that day or the next. Well, I always knew honesty pays and gives a blessing. This proves it again."

Lester was made manager of the carpet department and had one full-time and three part-time employees working for him. His department did extremely well. When rooms in customers' houses needed to be measured for carpets, he was the one who went and he took samples with him so they could see how the colors went with their paint and furniture. Sometimes he did some of this work in his spare time during the evening.

Soon after Lester started working there, an eighteen-year-old woman approached him and said, "I see you pray before you eat your lunch at noon. Would you please pray for my sister?"

"What's her problem?" asked Lester.

"Her husband left her," she explained with tears running down her cheeks. "She's had a hard life and just recently had a nervous breakdown. She just could not take all the pressure anymore and is in the hospital. The two little children are at my parents' home."

"Do you believe in prayer?" asked Lester. "Did you pray for her? Do your parents pray?"

"Yes," she said rather slowly. "I think they did a few times—not every day."

At lunchtime that day Lester invited her to join him. They held hands and prayed for her sister and the husband. Before leaving for home they prayed again. "I learned the power of prayer long before I was your age," he told her.

When Lester saw her the next morning, he asked her how things were going with her sister.

"The nurse said she rested better last night," was her reply.

Lester and the young woman prayed together three times that day. He also prayed several times while working during the day.

The next day she came to his department as soon as he was in. She was so happy she gave Lester a big hug with tears of love in her eyes saying, "My sister's husband came to visit her in the hospital last evening. He is willing to come back to live with her and the family again. They cried together last night. He told my sister something took place the other day at work. He doesn't know what it was, but he wants to start going to church again.

"Oh, I'm so glad we prayed together, especially for the sake of her little children. They couldn't understand where daddy was," she thankfully said to Lester.

"Tell your parents to pray every day from now on and perhaps he will always love her," advised Lester. "It doesn't cost one cent to pray, but going out to see a show or playing sports soon costs you lots of money."

Another Job

In 1973 Lester was offered a job as manager of a carpet store. He was undecided whether or not to leave Gimbels, since he liked working there. The other store owner had heard about Lester's reputation of knowing how to make sales, and they needed more business to keep out of debt.

He accepted the job and was working there only a few months when his baby boy was born and died. Later, the owner of the store offered Lester and Betty a free vacation in Florida due to their loss. They rented a car, saw the highlights of Florida, and visited Betty's relatives at Lake Worth. They agreed it had been a wonderful trip.

Shortly after he returned to work at the carpet store, Lester was asked to stand close to the front of the store and keep an eye on a new salesman. If customers did not buy or order anything from him, Lester was to approach them before they left the store and ask if they needed any help or information.

The owner had noticed that his sales had dropped while Lester was on vacation. He knew that if he wanted to show a profit on his books, he needed satisfied customers who kept coming back.

Lester evaluated the situation and felt the company needed some hints on how to run a business. They had a good line of carpets, but he sensed their sales were not managed properly. He had seen this a few times at other places where he worked and could tell the business was headed into debt.

"The more educated the salesmen are, the less honest they are," he thought. "Weren't they taught the Golden Rule *(Do unto others as you would have them do unto you)*? It seems that everybody who operates a business only thinks about making a lot of money as soon as possible. Do they really think no one will notice their crooked business? Must they always learn the hard way?

"One thing I know," he said to himself "if they had a teacher like the last one I had, I don't need to wonder why things go flop for some of these firms. They were only taught the knack of doing it the dishonest or unfair way and lying to get by." Then he added, "But there are also many who aren't like that."

Lester noticed that the fellow who went to measure customers' rooms for jobs was ordered to not give estimates on the price. He turned in his figures at the office and a secretary called the customer with the installed price of the carpet they wanted.

If the customer felt the cost was too high and mentioned they wanted to look elsewhere, Lester was sent out to take another measurement. He was to tell the folks the first man hadn't turned in the correct figures, give them an adjusted price, and tell them the men would be there to install the carpet on a certain date. If the customer said they didn't want it, Lester was to pretend he hadn't heard.

Three different sales slips were made up for each job:

one for the installer with the right amount of carpet needed; another slip for the buyer with his price on it; and then another slip with an adjusted price for the office. After the carpet was laid and the job done, the bill sent to the customer was much more than what the slip Lester had given them showed.

Lester hated that practice because although he didn't lie to the customer, the company made it look as though he did. The customers often declared, "We'll never buy from that company again." The dishonesty bothered him more and more and before long he had difficulty sleeping at night.

The business wasn't bringing in the money the owner hoped for and he called Lester to the office. "Lester, you must work harder and do the selling the way I tell you to. We won't get out of debt this way. You must be smarter than the buyer. Do you understand?"

"Yes, I understand," Lester said feeling righteous anger. "You want to make a liar out of me. Two-thirds of what you say are lies, and I'm telling you now, you won't stay in business very long unless you try a different method. I've worked for guys like you before and it never works. Sooner or later you will go bankrupt, then you'll think of what I told you. I've advised people before and the ones who took my advice thanked me later.

"Honesty pays," snapped Lester. "Look it up in the dictionary. Know how to spell it? H O N E S T Y!"

Taking the keys that belonged to the store from his pocket, he dropped them on the desk and said, "I can't work for a liar one more day. I quit!"

"Listen, the only men that leave here are the ones I fire. You can't quit without giving me a week's notice," stormed the boss.

Lester repeated, "I quit," and walked out the door.

It was with mixed emotions that he drove home. He knew he was right to follow his conscience, but what was Betty going to say when he got home without a job?

Satan is always ready to strike a blow after a battle is won, and Lester started feeling depressed. "Why didn't God let me stay out in the woods by the still waters? There I wouldn't have had to face all these wrong dealings. It was so peaceful out there—no arguing, cheating, or having to tell people that they are dishonest. I don't make enough money to live on by just selling tombstones."

God was also with him and soon he was remembering the good things. "Anyway, I surely am not lonely anymore like I was in the woods. I have a good wife and home and my life is full, working with people to help them be happy and honest. Thank You, God, and lead me where You want me."

By the time he got home, he was ready to look for another job immediately.

Working at Gimbels Again

Betty was amazed when he told her he had quit his job. "You quit without another job lined up?" she asked.

"Yes, I'll go back to Gimbels again. Wish I had never gone to the carpet store these four months."

That evening he went into Gimbels and saw no one in the carpet department except a saleswoman. He asked the manager of the furniture department who was working in the carpet department. "Only Sandy," was the reply. "The manager is in his office if you want to see him."

"Well, Lester Getz, how are you?" the manager greeted him. "Looking for a job, are you?"

"Will you take me back?"

"Sure will." His beaming smile showed his desire to have Lester back again. "We missed you in here. Some days are absolutely dull. You can start working tomorrow morning. Tell you what, my friend, I am giving you a $45 per week raise for coming back."

He continued, "You know Park City is open Sundays now, but you may have off Sunday and Monday. I know you are a Sunday school teacher and don't want to work Sundays."

The employees had always enjoyed Lester's sense of humor and the interesting things he had to talk about at lunchtime, so they were glad to see him back again.

His second week back he started a prayer circle of any employee who wished to attend. Usually 20 people showed up. One morning the manager asked, "May I join in the circle?"

The answer was, "Yes."

After the opening prayer, everyone had a chance to mention a special need to pray about. The manager said, "My mother-in-law is in the hospital. She is not able to go back to her home after she is released. She needs to decide whether to live with us or go to a nursing home. She's having a hard time deciding for herself."

The group continued to pray about the manager's concern, and then one morning he said, "My mother-in-law has decided to move in with us. We will take care of her and look after her needs. I know she will like it with us. Thanks for praying about the case." Then he added, "Sure glad you came back, Lester."

Lester worked at Gimbels until he retired at age 65.

※❀※

Another Phase of Life

Lester felt he could keep himself busy without getting another full-time job. He wanted to spend more of his time in church activities, and he was still selling memorials five days a week, by appointment. For that business he opened a showroom at the corner of East Lincoln Avenue and Cedar Street in Lititz.

He did not want to neglect his church duties because of business, so the showroom was closed Sunday and Monday. God came first in his life—he didn't want to honor God with only his leftover time.

One Saturday a woman came in and picked out a special tombstone which she liked. She asked the price, but wanted time to think about it first. "I might shop around a bit," she said.

"Well, you are welcome to shop around anywhere you like," said Lester. "I will be open on Tuesday again, but you can call me on Monday to set an appointment. I'm not open to customers Sunday or Monday."

Early Sunday morning the phone rang. Lester and Betty were just leaving for Sunday school and church. It was the lady saying she was coming over soon to buy that tombstone.

Lester answered, "We are going to church and I make no sales on Sunday. I told you yesterday, remember?"

On Monday she called again. "I was at Allentown yesterday and that one store had the same tombstone you have, but I had to pay $200 more for it there. It seems to me," she added, "that he said he gets the tombstones from you, so I figured you would give me back the $200 difference. Will you send it to me or must I come and get it? I work every day except Sunday, so I had to do my business yesterday. I guess you understand."

"Yes, I understand," remarked Lester. "But you did not buy it here in my store, so I do not owe you the $200 difference. Do you realize that it cost you $200 for not going to church on Sunday? You work five or six days a week and then lose half of your wages by not honoring God on Sunday. He wants you to keep His day holy. Didn't your parents teach you that?"

"Well, yes," she stammered, "but you know things are different now. We hardly can afford to do things during the week and not work every day, so Sundays is a good day to get caught after. If you are not willing to give me the $200, we'll make out."

"Look, lady," answered Lester over the phone, "people might be different now from what they were when you were a child, but God is not different, neither is His son Jesus. If you go to church every Sunday, He will bless you. Otherwise, you will lose more money by doing business on Sunday. Do you believe that?"

"Maybe. Could be some truth in that, but since my husband passed away, I can hardly keep my bills paid."

"If you honor His Word, God will pay them for you in ways you don't expect by giving you a blessing," advised Lester.

He spoke from experience. Although he lost some sales over the years by not selling on Sunday, the Lord blessed him in many ways.

After 13 years, at age 78, he gave up his showroom and

retired again. He had sold memorials for 41 years. From the age of ten, when he hired himself out to Joe Hurst, until he was 78 he had worked and supported himself. He had put in long hours and often worked beyond a 40-hour work week. He had also never drawn an unemployment check. His enjoyment of work had often led him to volunteer his services free for the satisfaction of helping others. As far as he knew, he had never cheated anyone. He had become acquainted with many interesting and sometimes difficult-to-love people. Always he tried to share something of value with each person he met.

✳✳✳

Retirement?

As Lester entered his retirement years, he hoped God could still use him. His only question was where and how. His motto was *Never refuse the work of the Lord*, so he prayed and asked Jesus for help and guidance on what that work would be for his remaining life.

One place he knew God wanted him to serve Him was in church work. He and Betty were members of the United Methodist Church where he was an usher and later the Sunday school superintendent. For a while he was chairman of the church board. Betty was the Christian partner he had yearned for in his younger years.

Betty's sister-in-law told them about a good evangelist who was speaking at a small church in Ephrata. The next evening they went to hear him preach and sat on a pew somewhere in the middle of the church. Before the services started, a young man came up behind Lester and tapped him on the shoulder. Lester looked around to see who it was.

The young man asked, "Do you remember me?"

"Well, your face looks familiar," said Lester.

"I am the pastor of this church. When I was a little boy, you often walked past our house Sunday mornings on your way to Sunday school. I always thought I wanted to be a good man like you when I grow up."

"Are you the boy who was at the window one Saturday night when I rushed out to rescue you and your mother? I've

100

never forgotten how I ran through that heavy rainstorm and how the door opened by itself when I wanted to enter your kitchen."

"Yes, that was me and my mother," he said.

"You know, I always wondered about that shrill voice I heard in my bedroom that told me I must go because there was someone there that I must save," said Lester. "Now I know why God hollered at me and made me go out and get drenching wet that night. It was to save one of His future servants. When I was coming to your house, I remembered how Christ had laid down His life for us, and I felt I had to be willing to do the same and maybe lay down my life for you or your mother. Now we are both brothers in Christ.

"So now you must do the same for anyone here in your church," Lester continued. "You may have to walk through some heavy storms to stay true to Christ, and even lay down your life by preaching repentance to people who don't want to repent."

Meeting and talking with that young man was an assurance to Lester that he had heard the voice of God. He was grateful that he had been obedient to His call.

After they moved to Lititz, Lester and Betty transferred their membership to the Lititz Church of God. He was soon active there as a Sunday school teacher and as a greeter of those arriving for services.

He taught his last Sunday school class on the day of his eightieth birthday. As long as his health permitted, he attended church regularly.

Lester and Betty were very active in church and religious activities in the early years of their retirement. They became acquainted with and involved in the Lebanon Full Gospel Christian Businessmen's group.

Lester was not a preacher but was one of the men who counseled people who went forward for prayer and advice at the end of the meetings. Once two young women came forward but stood back rather shyly. Lester's friend, John, who was another counselor, went up to them and said, "I will pray for you, and Lester here will pray in the Spirit."

Lester's reaction was: "God, not me! I never received that Holy Spirit gift." Then to his amazement and awe, when he opened his mouth, the words just flowed. He did not understand or remember one word he said, but the women told him afterward that they understood what he was saying and it was exactly what they needed to hear to make them understand about salvation. They both accepted Christ that night after they understood how Jesus died for their sins. It was something they had never grasped until the Holy Spirit put the Holy Spirit language into Lester's mouth.

The counselors would try to get all new Christians connected with a good church, The women did not know where to go, so John advised them to go to a church where he knew there was a good pastor. Both joined the church as did the husband of one of the women. The other husband wasn't sure at that time and wanted more time to think about it.

Lester thanked the Lord for these three converts and was grateful that he was allowed to be God's servant to lead them to Christ. He wanted to be ready and available to help anyone who asked him advice about being a Christian, but he didn't believe in going door to door preaching to people who weren't ready or interested in the things of God. He felt that type of action often destroyed relationships and sometimes forced people into promises that were not true worship of God. He also felt God would lead him to the ones who would benefit from hearing the advice and counsel he could give them out of his life of hardship and faithfulness to God.

Lester and Betty and their friends, John and Mabel, spent their spring and fall vacations at PTL in Charlotte, North Carolina. It was a place where they could hear good speakers and musical groups, and where there was a ministry which gave Christian counsel to people over the telephone. John and Lester were sometimes on the counseling phones for hours. Their wives enjoyed the meetings and visiting with new friends from many different states.

After Lester's eightieth birthday, he lost sight in one eye. His doctor sent him to an eye specialist. There he was informed that sight in one eye was gone and the other eye was bad. A retina specialist told him the same thing. The laser treatment he received didn't improve his vision and in January of 2002 his doctor declared him legally blind, although he can still see a little.

He also noticed his hearing in one ear was fading after he turned eighty. He then lost the use of one arm. A few years later he realized he could hardly smell anymore. He has tried to be patient through the losses due to an aging body, but he loves to visit with people and often tells them the stories told here.

When he was hospitalized in 2002 with lung problems, the doctor diagnosed emphysema and put him on oxygen 24 hours a day. The oxygen supports his labored breathing. He also uses a nebulizer four times a day which puts medication in his lungs.

Lester says, "God never causes our sickness, but He allows Satan to test us. This way he knows how strong our faith is in Him. God is always near to keep us strong and not allow Satan to lead us astray." But he will add, "Keep God in your hearts at all times so you are ready when the day comes to go to that mansion which God has prepared for us."

Lester reached his ninetieth birthday on May 23, 2003. He was looking forward to the day when his wife Betty could read this book to him—the story of his life compiled from talks with a friend and the notes Betty had written. We believe God gave us help from above to understand and write this book and He alone deserves the honor. Lester prays that his hard life and experiences of putting God first will help many people better understand the way of salvation and faith.

Lester and Betty live in a small house in Lititz. He does not want to go to a nursing home, and Betty wants to care for him in spite of all his health problems. It is quite a strain, for she is not young and strong anymore either.

Why does she care for him? Betty says, "Because I love him as much as the day we were married. I want to do for him whatever he asks. This is what I promised before God nearly 35 years ago." What a faithful wife and promise!

Lester's advice to you is: "A real Christian does not retire or get tired of hearing God's Word. Someday I hope to hear God tell me that I have fought a good fight and kept the faith."

End of Lester's story.

Scared by a Hobo (Tramp)

The Jacob Miller family (the author's grandparents) lived at the corner of West Eby and Mill Creek Roads in the area of Leola, Pennsylvania, a mile from Christ Lapp's farm. William Getz (a brother to Samuel) lived at the end of their lane in their tenant house. No doubt William helped Jacob with the harvest, as that was often part of the agreement when renting a tenant house.

When Jacob's daughter, Rachel (the author's mother), was seven years old, she worked a few days a week as a hired girl for Christ and Lavina Lapp. Lester's family lived in Lapps' tenant house. I can well remember my mother talking about the Getz families, but I can't recall Mother ever talking of Lester Getz. Lester, however, remembers one day in May when he and Christ came to the house for dinner and there was a shy little Amish girl there putting the things on the table. Lavina had said, "Lester, this is our little hired girl, Rachel Miller."

My mother also related how the Lapps were quite generous folks and how she enjoyed working for them and did whatever she was told to do.

When the wild blackberries were ripe, Rachel was told to go pick some along the fence rows. One day Lavina told her she would find some among the bushes and trees out by the railroad tracks at the far end of the fields.

She was cautiously searching the thorny bushes for ripe berries when she suddenly spied a hobo (tramp) walking along the railroad tracks toward her. The joy of picking berries faded as she realized she was all alone and no one would hear her if she cried out. She was not used to meeting strangers except in the presence of her parents, so she carefully squatted down hoping the man had not noticed her.

Shivering with fear and with racing heartbeats, she held herself motionless barely breathing. She prayed earnestly and silently to God for His protection and that the man would not see or harm her.

She didn't relax or stand up until the hobo had passed and even then she was almost too afraid to peek down the tracks to be sure that he was gone. Then another fear rose up. What if another one came by?

It was hard to pick berries and watch up and down the railroad track at the same time, and her little berry pail was only half full when she judged it was time to return to the farmhouse.

Tears trickled down her cheeks as she told Lavina about her scary afternoon and explained why she hadn't picked more berries.

Kindhearted Lavina said, "You poor darling, you did not need to stay out there and keep on picking with such a fear."

"But I wanted to fill the pail as you told me to. My mother told me if I'm a hired girl I shall do as Lavina says," Rachel replied.

"You told me to stay off the railroad tracks so no train would hit me, and I did. I was afraid to sing in case another tramp came by, so I prayed to God instead."

"Yes, you were a brave little girl to depend on God's protection. I am sorry I forgot to tell you about the tramps who walk along the tracks. But did you know most of them are good people and God takes care of them too?" Lavina said. "The next time we will go picking blackberries together.

"Those men depend mostly on farmers' wives for their food and we let them sleep in our barn at night. They seldom harm children. Many of them had little children of their own at one time."

Lavina was a good homemaker and kept her house clean, her garden neat, and her lawn beautiful with many flowers.

Spring cleaning didn't stop inside a house. After the house was cleaned from top to bottom, the outside got spruced up also. It was the custom with most families to whitewash fence posts, tree trunks, and any brick wall around the house or barnyard. The trees were whitewashed to the same height as the fence posts. Whitewash was made by mixing powdered lime and water in a bucket. The white solution was applied with a short-handled brush. Each housewife hoped to be the first in the neighborhood to get this work done and no doubt harbored a bit of pride in her heart when she viewed the finished job.

One rather cold spring day Lavina said, "Well, Rachel, it's time to get the whitewashing done."

Rachel mixed the solution and started brushing on the white mixture. Her hands grew colder and colder and soon she noticed the solution in her bucket was becoming icy, but she kept on with her job. Once more Lavina apologized for the discomfort she had caused her hired girl who was then 14 years old.

When Lester's life changed so dramatically, he often remembered those days at the Lapp farm and wished he could return to them. He remembered Lavina's pretty flowers and also the little Amish girl. Both he and Rachel were too bashful to talk to each other. Smiles were enough.

Rachel kept on working for Lapps into her teenage years. She proved to be a faithful hired girl who still obeyed whatever orders Lavina gave.

The hobo who scared Rachel was just one of many men who roamed the country before and during the Great Depression. They crisscrossed the country seeking work. Many walked, but some stole rides on top of or under railroad cars. Some had families they were sending money home to, but many had deserted their families when they had lost their jobs. They carried all their earthly possessions in small packs on their backs. They were usually courteous and ate whatever a housewife put on the plate for them. Some people invited them to share a meal at their table, but usually they ate their handouts on the porch steps. Before a farmer would allow them to sleep in his barn, he usually asked for any matches they might be carrying. He didn't want them smoking and burning down his buildings.

When Hobos Walked the Roads

After the Great Depression began in 1929 with the United States stock market crash, many people were out of work. Many businesses became bankrupt. This caused hard times and money was very scarce, not only for the poor day laborer, but also for wealthy businessmen, lawyers, doctors, engineers, etc., who were left penniless and with big debts.

With no money to support their families, many men left their homes and took to the roads. Some never saw their wife and children again. Their wives tried to keep the children fed and clothed with whatever little income they and the children could earn.

This was before Social Security benefits or old age retirement plans. Some who had been in the Armed Forces in their younger years received pension checks once a month. This was a small amount of cash for these men who were called bums or hobos or tramps. The dictionary defines all three words as a person who wanders from place to place doing odd jobs or spends most of his time loafing or begging.

As a small country boy in the 1940's, living at home with my parents, I well remember some of these men who walked the road carrying a small pack on their shoulders.

A few parents scared their children by telling them these men were dangerous, but very few were. Many mothers taught their children that the men would not hurt them. They reminded their children that Jesus also had no home and that if they were kind to the homeless men, it would bring a blessing and they themselves would not become poor through sharing what food they had. Most often the hobos were courteous when they walked up a farm lane, knocked at the door of a farmhouse, and asked the missus, "Do you have any work I could do for something to eat?"

"Yes," was the common reply for quite often the housewife asked the hobo to chop a certain amount of wood before he ate. "Then just wait outside on the porch when you are finished."

Many folks burned firewood to heat their house in winter and to cook in summer, so this was a good way to get the firewood chopped. The men who had regular routes soon knew how the folks at each place preferred to have their wood split and stacked.

Hobos walked the rural roads east of the Appalachians long before the Depression years. Many housewives had seen their mothers and grandmothers handing out meals any time of day. These women were not afraid of the hobos, because their parents had taught them to treat the men as if Jesus was knocking on their door. As the Holy Word reads, "Inasmuch as you have done unto one of these, you have done unto me."

Most Amish and many of the other plain people considered it a sacred thing to share with the homeless who walked the road begging.

Some hobos had lived rich lives prior to the Great Depression. The loss of jobs, homes, and families caused many to feel defeated. Those who had been involved in drinking liquor before, often practiced that bad habit whenever they had any money. This was a shameful way of spending their money, and, for that reason, most people refused to give them money but willingly provided a plate of food.

The hobo had few personal possessions. Shoes were perhaps their most valuable personal property because of the walking they did every day. They kept their luggage as light as possible. The packs, carried over their shoulders, contained little more than an extra shirt and pair of trousers. A long, heavy coat and a narrow-brim hat were almost the uniform of the hobo and were often worn summer and winter.

Some of the hobos followed a set route which brought them to the same house every four, five, or six weeks. They remembered which housewife served good meals and also those who only gave a sandwich and a cup of black coffee.

They all seemed to like very strong coffee.

I remember a few times when one was already sitting out on our porch eating and another one knocked on the door begging for a meal. We knew they were not friends, because they did not sit side-by-side. "Thanks, missus," was the only tip ever given.

When the meal was finished, the hobo left the plate and cup on the porch, without further disturbing the housewife, and walked off. Few left any food on their plate and they were not choosy about what they were given.

Some women fed five or six hobos a week. Some came at supper time and asked to stay and sleep in the barn overnight. Most smoked pipes or cigars and carried barn-burner matches. Farmers always asked for these matches before granting the men a place to bed down on the soft hay in their barn. The hobo knew that was the policy of anyone wishing to sleep in the barn because of the dry hay and usually complied without hesitation. I remember seeing one on his knees praying aloud, before going to sleep. Some of these men had a form of religion.

The next morning while the farmer was milking his cows by hand, the hobo would come for his matches and thank the farmer for his free lodging. If not invited to stay for breakfast, they went on to another farm. They did not stop at every farm, but if they were close to one where they knew good meals were served, they would sit on a bank by the road waiting. When they figured a meal might be prepared for the family, they walked up the lane and knocked on the door hoping for a nice plate of leftovers.

As with all kinds of people, some were quite friendly, some were bold, some were willing to help a farmer with his harvest of hay and wheat, and some were lazy. At times it was difficult to judge if a man was telling the truth or telling lies.

The first hobo I remember was Jimmy. When I was perhaps seven years old, he complained of aches and pains of arthritis and asked my mother for her rubbing alcohol before retiring in the barn at night. She gave him the pint bottle, three-fourths full. Near noontime the next day, Jimmy appeared at the door and asked for his matches. Mother asked him where the bottle of alcohol was. He said, "I used it all. The bottle is empty." Mother suspected he drank it and wasn't able to get up earlier. Other hobos schemed the same way to get alcohol if they were awful thirsty.

Another hobo of my childhood years was one folks called *Base Bill* (mad Bill). Perhaps he had a habit of getting mad, although I don't remember. He came to my parents every four weeks on Sunday morning. Evidently he knew which Sunday dads attended church and when they would be home. Mother often gave him a big bowl of coffee soup, the same as our family had for Sunday breakfast.

Occasionally neighbor women talked about a certain hobo. They sensed some hobos had two breakfast meals on the same morning. I never remember a fat hobo nor do I remember any that were awfully skinny. They ate whenever they could get a meal, but they also walked many miles.

One fellow earned the name President. He was very bold and outspoken. He must have been educated, because he read the newspaper and seemed to know all about politics and news from around the globe. Of course, he might just have been bragging or lying, because there on the farm we did not know any world news back in the 1940's.

My grandmother, who lived in the retirement end of our farmhouse, was very good to President. If the weather was cold, she invited him into the washhouse to eat his supper rather than sit outside on the concrete steps.

He came around every two weeks and Grandma decided she would ask him to pay fifteen cents for every meal, if he came that often. He was actually quite pleased to sit on a chair and order what he wanted. She then allowed him to eat inside at the end of the kitchen sink.

Sad to say, President teased and tormented my Uncle Benny who was mentally handicapped. Benny did not like that bold, gruff-voiced hobo who thought he knew everything.

President received a pension check which he had mailed to my Uncle Sammy's address. Uncle Sammy enjoyed chatting with him and many times allowed him to sleep in his feed entry. If I recall right, he was found dead there one morning. No one knew who or where his family or relatives lived. Someone came and picked up the body and that was the last I heard about him.

Another hobo in my youth was Jack Donaho. He was a good worker and farmers hired him quite often. He helped my dad harvest hay, wheat, and tobacco. Since he was a hired man, he was allowed to eat at our table where we found his body odor quite strong. He, at least, was one hobo who seldom took a bath.

Later he worked for an Amish farmer and lived in his tobacco stripping room a few years. Folks trusted and respected him until one day while the farmer and his family were away, Jack and the farmer's wallet disappeared.

I was the hired boy on that farm when nearly six months later Jack came walking through the fields where the farmer and I were working. Jack patted my boss on the shoulder and started telling him what a nice guy he was.

"Ha, ha," laughed the farmer, "you deserve to like me if you took my pocketbook and all the money. Aren't you gonna thank me for it?"

Another hobo I remember from the late 1950's was a man with bushy white hair. He didn't shave. He had a mustache and beard plus hair down to his shoulders. I don't know if we knew what his correct name was, but my folks called him the Long-Haired Tramp. Hobos were often given names that somehow described their character or appearance.

Uncle Sammie Fisher was a humorous fellow and he named the long-haired tramp Christ (*Grisht Ebersol*). Uncle Sammie would say, "Hi, *Grisht*. Ain't so, you're *Grisht Ebersol*?" The hobo didn't mind if he called him by that name.

Once over the Christmas holidays he spent two days and nights lying on his bed of soft hay in my dad's feed entry. Mother taught us children to respect the hobos and treat them kindly. She said, "We will think of this old man as being like Jesus who was born out in a stable and was found lying on the hay on Christmas morning." She served him roast turkey and all the goodies of a Christmas dinner. What a nice remembrance of my mother's teaching.

This seventy-year-old hobo craved attention, and one method to get some was to pretend he was sick or not feeling well. He would then ask to stay a day or two at one farm. If the farmer mentioned about getting a doctor, the long-haired hobo soon moved on to the another farm down the road and tried to play the same scheme there. When the Amish and Mennonites visited on Sunday afternoons, they occasionally talked about the hobos who had stopped at their places and so learned some of their tricks.

In 1973 my wife and I moved our family onto a farm of 60 acres along Peters Road, three miles south of New Holland, Pennsylvania. We began farming there with a family of five children, ages one and one-half to ten years. Only one hobo, Bill Murphy, came to our farm then—possibly three times a year begging for a meal and to sleep in our barn at night.

By the 1970's few children knew anything about hobos, but ours had a chance to get a glimpse of the hobo lifestyle.

One cold December day Bill was in our tobacco stripping room all day while my wife and I stripped tobacco. It was a treat for him to sit on an upside-down five-gallon bucket beside the wood stove.

As we worked he told us about his life of walking the road. I remember only a few of the stories he related.

Many years before when he lost his job, he tried to get work, but nothing was available. His wife left him when he had no money to pay the rent and care for their two children. The children became undernourished and someone took them from him. They were put into a children's home.

Bill then followed the trend of many men and walked the road begging for his meals. His responsibilities were few. He had more to eat than before, but he lost total contact of his two children. When I knew him, he had no idea where they were or what had become of them.

For over 30 years he walked the road all up and down the eastern seaboard. He soon learned in which territories he went hungry and where he could expect to be welcomed. In some areas where he was not known he met with some harsh treatment. Mostly he stopped among the plain folks who were farmers and he was seldom turned away hungry.

In his younger years Bill wandered wherever his interest took him. The last ten years of walking he stayed mostly in Lancaster County where he could depend on good meals from farmers' wives and overnight lodging in a farmer's barn.

Once he walked in a driveway and saw a big German shepherd dog tied on the porch. He estimated the length of the chain and decided the dog could not reach the door. The second Bill knocked on the door, however, the dog sprang at him and bit him on the arm. After the one bite, the dog backed away and began to bark.

Blood was dripping out of his coat sleeve when the front door opened. With the pain increasing, Bill stuttered, "Your dog bit my arm."

The man looked at him, saw the dripping blood, and snapped, "That's what he's here for." With that, the door slammed shut.

Bill hurried down the lane and up the road. If his memory was correct and he was on the right road, there was a lady nearby who had been friendly to him before. Soon he recognized a little bridge and then a white tobacco shed along the road.

Friendly Amish children were playing in the yard as he strode toward the house. They continued their play and showed they were not afraid of him. When he knocked on the door, one little seven-year-old girl spoke up, "Mother is out in the garden in back of the house, I'll go tell her."

A lady in a purple dress and with streaks of sweat on her sun-bronzed face came around the side of the house. She greeted him kindly. "Hi, are you hungry?"

"Yes," Bill replied, "but I need someone to take care of my arm." He then told her what happened.

"Oh, some dogs are terrible," she said as she hurried him into the laundry room and gathered soap, water, salve, and bandages. "I would not have a dog like that on my property.

Now let me see how it looks."

Bill took off his coat and she rolled up his filthy dirty shirt sleeve.

"My, oh my, this looks bad. I'll get you a few aspirins to relieve the pain." She carefully washed his arm with a wash cloth and warm soapy water while her four youngsters watched wide-eyed and silent.

"Maybe we should go to the doctor and have this stitched," she continued, "but for now I think I'm just gonna put plenty of this healing salve on and wrap it well."

Bill watched as the plump, Good Samaritan lady bandaged his arm just as though she was caring for her own child. "Now don't go far out of the area in case you need to come back to have it bandaged again." She said as she hurried to prepare a platter of food for him.

"She gave me a good meal of mashed potatoes and gravy bread, plus cooked carrots and a big piece of cake and a cup of coffee," Bill told my wife and me that day in the stripping room. "And do you know what else she gave me? A ten-dollar bill to pay for a doctor in case my arm got infected later on. She sure was a nice lady. I thanked her for it and she said, 'You're quite welcome, come again and God bless you.'"

Bill left the bandage on for over a week. Then when the arm started getting itchy he took it off and the arm was nearly healed. "I spent the ten dollars to buy a pair of used shoes at a reduced-price store," he said.

"You can hardly believe how different people are. Some, like that man who owned the dog, wouldn't care if I got killed," he said.

I told Bill that perhaps some mothers never teach their children to treat poor folks kindly. Some only show respect to the rich and mighty.

Another incident Bill told us that day was about when he was in a strange area. As he walked, he got hungry, but there were no farms along the road, just occasional houses. Finally, he saw farm buildings at quite a distance. The wash hanging on a line told him the people were not plain folks.

He hoped these folks weren't the type that would give

him a scanty meal or refuse to open the door to his knock. Occasionally some women hid themselves and had the children stay quiet until the hobo gave up and left the property.

At this house, however, a man answered the door. "Yes, I'll get a sandwich ready, but you wait 'til we're done with our dinner."

A half-hour later the door opened again and the man said, "Here is your sandwich, but don't eat it here on our property. Will you promise to go down the road at least a mile to eat it?"

"Ye-s-s," said Bill a bit confused at such a strange command. "Quite weird," he thought as he walked away.

When he assumed he was a mile from the house, he sat under a shade tree, shed his coat and hat, and without a glance inside the bread began to eat his scanty meal.

His afternoon nap on the dry grass was soon interrupted with severe stomach pains. This was very unusual for a man who was used to eating any kind of food.

The pain increased rapidly. He couldn't throw up, and when he decided to work off the pain, by walking, he found he was so dizzy he had to lie down. Sweat broke out all over his body as the intestinal pain increased. Soon he came to a bridge and crept under it to cool off. When he tried to walk again, he was so dizzy he fell.

Bill was sure he would die and was convinced the man had put spoiled meat or perhaps poison in his sandwich. "That was why he ordered me off his property before eating the sandwich. He figured no one could blame him for the murder if I was found dead somewhere else."

He committed himself to God and hoped He will allow him to enter heaven after death.

He longed for a drink of clean water or that someone might find him and take him to a doctor. Holding perfectly still was the only way he had to relieve his pain that night.

The next morning he sat up a bit, but as soon as he began to move the awful pain struck him down flat again. He wanted to get a few sips of water from the stream to quench his thirst, but the dizziness kept him lying flat. For two days and nights

Bill stayed under the bridge enduring such terrible stomach pain that he sometimes passed out. He thought he would die and perhaps no one would ever find his body. Cows passed under the bridge and drank from the stream and they might eventually trample his body into the mud. Finally, the pain let up enough that he was able to rest.

Very weak and exhausted he started walking again, The next farmhouse he came to had a horse and carriage tied at the barn so he decided to trust these people.

His hope was fulfilled when after explaining his painful experience to the lady he saw a sparkle of love in her eyes. She gave him a bottle of Pepto-Bismol and said, "Take three tablespoonful of this, while I fix you a soft meal of soup. We don't want your stomach to flare up again."

After he ate his meal slowly, she said, "You take the bottle of medicine with you just in case you feel bad again after this meal."

It is hard for me to believe a man would treat a homeless man that way even if he was wearing dirty clothing and begging for food. The hobos of the past surely cost our government very little compared to all the people living off unemployment and welfare checks today. But such is life. Some people hate and others love the very same person. But God loves them all. The Holy Word says, "Love ye one another."

Another rough experience happened to Bill when he was taking a shortcut using a man's field lane to get to a farmhouse he knew. He was tired and hungry and looking forward to a meal of perhaps ham, mashed potatoes and gravy, home-canned peaches, and maybe even fresh, homemade bread. The lady of that farmhouse always served him very good meals.

The owner of the land where he was walking the field lane was out in his field cultivating corn that warm July afternoon. When he came to the end of the row he opened the cab door of his air-conditioned, diesel tractor and shouted, "What are you doing on my property. You no-good rascal."

"I'm only using your field lane to get over to the next farm," answered Bill.

117

"Well in the name of the Pennsylvania law, I tell you to get off my property right now."

"Okay, I will, sir."

"Well then get off right now," he shouted harshly.

Bill picked up speed, but the farmer pulled his tractor up beside Bill and continued to yell, "I said, get off RIGHT NOW."

"I will as fast as I can," said Bill feeling all shook up. He was nearly running.

"RIGHT NOW, I said," he repeated as he drove almost at Bill's heels.

Then Bill stopped and said, "I'm sorry sir, but I can't fly."

The farmer yelled again, "Don't ever come on my land again," and throttled up his tractor creating a fearful noise. Bill feared he was going to drive right over him with that big tractor.

Bill was nearly 70 years old at that time and he was careful to avoid ever stepping on that property again.

I had to think of the Bible story of the rich man and Lazarus. Surely the women who served good meals and gave Bill medicine and bandaged his arm received blessings for their good deeds. God alone is the judge, but I can't help but wonder what rewards or lack of blessings were reaped by the cruel farmer and the man who gave him spoiled or poisoned food.

My wife and I were deeply touched when Bill talked about a very good friend of his, an Amish woman who was related to us. He showed us his heavy woolen sweater. She had given it to him as a Christmas gift the year before. When we told him she had since passed away, he remarked sadly, "That woman was my best friend."

As Bill sat beside our warm stove all day relating his life, I thought, "I never want to complain again when things don't go as I plan," but I must admit I have failed to keep that pledge many, many times. I must remind myself of it and never give up trying, however.

The Depression years lasted from 1929 to 1940. No doubt

some of the road walkers could have applied for a job after the Great Depression was over, but many had lost track of their wives and families. They preferred to stay on the road, work when they had to, live a life free of responsibilities, and get free meals and lodging wherever they could find them. Surely their lives were often lonely.